Ancient Peoples and Places

THE MONGOLS

General Editor

DR.GLYN DANIEL

ABOUT THE AUTHOR

Born in Altrincham, England, in 1910, E. D. Phillips studied classics and humanities at Westminster School, London, and Christ Church, Oxford. During most of his life, he has taught classics at various universities; he is currently teaching at the Queen's University of Belfast, in Northern Ireland. He is a Fellow of the Society of Antiquaries and of the Royal Anthropological Institute and the author of The Royal Hordes: Nomad Peoples of the Steppes.

Ancient Peoples and Places

THE
MONGOLS

E. D. Phillips

39 PHOTOGRAPHS
29 LINE DRAWINGS
3 MAPS

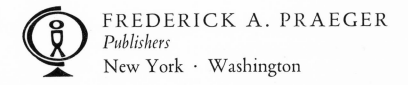

FREDERICK A. PRAEGER
Publishers
New York · Washington

THIS IS VOLUME SIXTY-FOUR IN THE SERIES
Ancient Peoples and Places
GENERAL EDITOR: DR. GLYN DANIEL

BOOKS THAT MATTER

Published in the United States of America in 1969
by Frederick A. Praeger, Inc., Publishers,
111 Fourth Avenue, New York, N.Y. 10003
© 1969 in London, England, by E. D. Phillips
All rights reserved
Library of Congress Catalog Card Number: 68–54309
Printed in Great Britain

CONTENTS

LIST OF ILLUSTRATIONS   7

PREFACE   10

AUTHOR'S NOTE   12

INTRODUCTION   13
   The Mongols in History : Sources of
   Information   13

 I THE MONGOLS AND THE NOMAD
    TRADITION   20

II CHINGIS KHAN   37
    The Rise of Chingis Khan   37
    The New Mongol State and Army   40
    The First Foreign Campaigns   51
    The Campaign in China   53
    The War against the Khwarazmshahs   57
    Jebe and Sübüdei in Caucasia and Russia   63
    The Tangut Campaign and the Death of
    Chingis   65
    Mukali in China   66
    Chingis Khan in History   67

III THE HEIRS OF CHINGIS KHAN   69
     Ögödei 1229–41   69

Güyük 1246–48   79
Möngke 1251–59   85

IV   THE SUCCESSOR STATES   104
    Kubilai and the Yüan Dynasty   104
    The Ilkhans in Iran   115
    The House of Jaghatai in Central Asia   125
    The Golden Horde on the Western Steppes   127

EPILOGUE   139

GENEALOGICAL TABLES   145

NOTES ON THE TEXT   150

BIBLIOGRAPHY   157

THE PLATES   161

NOTES ON THE PLATES   193

INDEX   198

ILLUSTRATIONS

PLATES

1 A Mongol horseman with game killed
2 Portrait of Chingis Khan
3 Temujin proclaimed Chingis Khan
4 Chingis Khan enthroned with Börtei
5 Chingis Khan receiving dignitaries
6 Inhabitants of Balkh leaving their city
7 Battle between armies of Chingis Khan and Jelal-ad-Din
8 Chingis Khan's encampment
9 Mongols besieging Chung-tu
10 The bier of Chingis Khan
11 Ogödei Khan and his sons Güyük and Kadan
12 The pavilion called Frashi at Karakorum
13 Portrait of Ögödei Khan
14 Portrait of the ageing Kubilai Khan
15 Kubilai Khan crossing a river
16 Hülegü feasts before invading Iran
17 Hülegü advances to attack the assassins
18 Hülegü besieges Baghdad
19 Mongols besieging a city on a river
20 Stampede of horses under fire
21 Prisoners led off by Mongol cavalry
22 Japanese champions Takezaki and the Ogano brothers attack Mongol warship

PLATES 23 Japanese attack another Mongol warship

24 Takezaki attacking Mongol archers

25 Cavalry pursuit

26 Tartar cavalry and orientals in combat

27 Hungarians and Tartars in battle on the Danube

28 Mongols pursuing King Bela of Hungary

29 Mongols with captive women

30 The Ilkhan Abaka and his son Arghun

31 Arghun with his family

32 The Ilkhan Gaikhatu Khan judges the generals

33 The Court of Ghazan Khan

34 The coffin of Ghazan Khan

35 Borak Khan recognized as ruler of the Jaghatai

36 Inscription in old Chinese seal character

37 Portrait of Khaishan Khan

38 Gold, silver and bronze coins of the thirteenth to eighteenth centuries AD

39 Defeat of Tokhta by Nogai

FIGURES 1 *Medieval Tartar huts and waggons, p. 29*

2 *A Mongol yurt, p. 31*

3 *Chingis Khan, p. 36*

4 *Chingis Khan with 'lot-casters', p. 39*

5 *Mongol warrior in scale armour, p. 43*

6 *Whistling arrow-heads, p. 44*

7 *Iron arrow-heads, p. 45*

8 *Weapons and gear, p. 46*

9 *Iron spear-heads and battle-axe, p. 47*

8

FIGURES   10   *Mongol warrior in lamellar armour, p. 48*

11   *Mongol archers, p. 49*

12   *Siege-engines, p. 50*

13   *Nakkaras or kettle-drums, p. 51*

14   *Map : Eastern Asia before the Mongol expansion,
p. 53*

15   *Map : Central and Western Asia and Russia
before the Mongol conquests, p. 59*

16   *Sübüdei, p. 64*

17   *Silver coin of Chingis Khan, p. 68*

18   *Batu Khan, p. 73*

19   *Mongol paitza, p. 77*

20   *Silver coin of the Great Khans, p. 78*

21   *Silver coin from regency of Queen Töregene, p. 79*

22   *Silver coin struck in the names of Güyük Khan
and David Narin, p. 80*

23   *Silver coin of Möngke, p. 89*

24   *Map : the Mongol Empire under the Great Khans,
pp. 92–3*

25   *Granite tortoise, p. 97*

26   *Cast-iron axle-boxes, iron sickle, p. 98*

27   *Pieces of iron cauldron, p. 98*

28   *Iron implements and utensils, p. 99*

29   *Plan of the Palace at Karakorum, p. 101*

30   *Bronze coin of the Yüan dynasty, p. 111*

31   *Bronze coin of Hülegü, p. 117*

32   *Gold coin of Ghazan Mahmud, p. 121*

Preface

M Y INTEREST IN THE Mongols began in boyhood, when I
read the account of them in H. G. Wells's *Outline of History*,
a book that was often condemned for ignoring some of the attitudes
usual among historians of its date. The gigantic scale and speed
of their operations in an age earlier than the invention of firearms
and of modern transport was always to me a matter of amaze-
ment. Since then, without having the Mongols specially in view,
I have made a study of all the great migrations and conquests of
the nomad peoples on the Northern Steppes and of the nomad
pattern of life. Without such an interest, it is difficult to see anything but the destructive aspect of Mongol history, which I have
certainly not passed over in the following pages. I have tried to
describe the age of Mongol power for itself and not just as a
ruinous interlude in Chinese, Iranian or Russian history.

In a series which is so largely concerned with archaeology, my
volume presents less than others of the material remains of the
people that it treats. That this could hardly be avoided will be
clear from the following considerations. The Mongols as nomads
on the Steppes have left much less that meets the eye than have
the Scythians or the Sarmatians with their distinctive art, and
they were careful to conceal all traces of their royal tombs. Under
their rule, civilized peoples continued to produce not only
literature but art and architecture too; these are, however, of
native origin and inspiration, though they owe much in some
cases to conditions brought about by the Mongol conquests.
Thus, while they are products of the Mongol period of their
respective cultures, they cannot be called Mongol work and
therefore do not fall to be illustrated here as such. For the age of
conquest and dominion with which we are concerned, Mongol
life is best illustrated archaeologically from the finds that came to

light on the sites of Karakorum in Mongolia and Berke Sarai by the Volga.

But in illustrating Mongol life, on the Steppes or elsewhere, we are not confined to archaeological material. There is also oriental art, Chinese and Persian, and some medieval art from Europe. Pictures, particularly in illuminated manuscripts, give a good idea of Mongol tents, dress, armour, weapons and horses, and have therefore been much used. These illustrations and the archaeological finds can be combined with the descriptions of Carpini, Rubruck and Marco Polo. They, as Europeans, found everything stranger than did other travellers and for our purposes observed it best. These sources together give a clearer view of Mongol life in the thirteenth and fourteenth centuries than might have been expected.

For help in the research and reading required for this book I am indebted particularly to Dr Basil Gray of the Department of Oriental Antiquities and to Mr N. M. Lowick of the Department of Coins and Medals in the British Museum, and also to Dr G. Frumkin of Geneva. I further acknowledge with thanks the assistance of the following persons or institutions: the Royal Asiatic Society and the Asiatic Society of Calcutta; the Warburg Institute; the Percival David Foundation of Chinese Art; the London Library; the Library of the School of Oriental and African Studies, University of London; the Bibliothèque Nationale; the Musée Guimet; the Stiftung Preussischer Kultur-besitz, through the Tübinger Depot der Staatsbibliothek; the Oesterreichische Nationalbibliothek; the National Szechenyi Library at Budapest; the Tokyo National Museum and the Vice-Grand-Chamberlain to H.I.M. the Emperor of Japan; Professor Shigeyasu Hasumi of Kyoto University; the Topkapi Sarayi Museum, Istanbul. I wish to extend my thanks to Mr T. R. Hardaker for his careful drawings of coins from the British Museum (Figs. 17, 19–23, 30, 31); also to Miss Gillian Jones for re-drawing Figs. 2, 6–12, 25–28 from the original sources, and to Mr S. Schotten for making the maps (Figs. 14, 15, 24) from my rough sketches. I am also much indebted for advice and criticism to the General Editor of the series, Dr Glyn Daniel, and to the staff of Thames and Hudson Ltd, who have given so much assistance with the maps and drawings.

E.D.P.

Author's Note

As far as possible, I have given to proper names and terms that are purely Mongol their Mongol forms, rather than those found in Chinese, Persian or Medieval European sources, which until recently it was customary to use. But for some well-known names these other spellings are given after the Mongol in brackets. In the spelling of Mongol names the English values of the letters and consonantal groupings used have as far as possible been kept.

VOWELS

a Long and short as in German or Italian (never English long *a* as in 'gate').

ö, ü Modified, as in German, since this sound is not used in English. (*ä* modified, as many scholars write it, has been reduced to *e*).

CONSONANTS AND CONSONANTAL GROUPS

ch As in English (= French *tch*, German *tsch* and professional orientalists' *č*).

j As in English (= French *dj*, German *dsch* and professional orientalists' *ǧ* or *ǰ*).

ng As in English 'finger': professional orientalists write this as *ngg*. At the end of a word I have left *ng* to sound as in 'ring'. (The velar gutteral *k* has been substituted for the *q* used by professional orientalists, since the distinction is not noticeable in English.) In transaction from Chinese I have followed the Wade-Giles system, except that I usually write *hs* as simple *h* in the middle of a name and as *s* at the beginning, e.g. *Hsi-Hsia* as *Si-Hia*, though for Hsiung Nu I have the familiar Hiung Nu, not Siung Nu.

Introduction

THE MONGOLS IN HISTORY: SOURCES OF INFORMATION

THIS BOOK IS NOT intended to be a complete history of the Mongol people from its origin down to modern times. The main theme can only be the achievements by which the Mongols earned their singular place in history: their conquests of the thirteenth century. But their origins must also be treated, and the later fates of the various kingdoms into which their empire was divided, so long as these were ruled by Mongol khans. The career of Timur, who was of Mongol descent but not of the imperial family, cannot be treated here for its own sake, though his impact on other Mongol kingdoms of his time will be noted. The total effect of such a narrative is to show the Mongol expansion as an irresistible torrent, which in the beginning swept uniformly over a great extent of the world, but later parted into local currents, steady at first but afterwards becoming slow and sluggish and drying eventually into pools and marshes of little account. The final chapter must return to the head-waters to follow briefly the more important of the changes that came about in the Mongolian homeland while the Russian and Chinese states acquired their modern territories. But the very latest history of Mongolia lies outside our subject: we are not concerned with the present Republic of Mongolia.

The theatre of events is enormous, for in the course of the thirteenth and fourteenth centuries the Mongol armies came to operate in various parts of an area that extended from Manchuria to Palestine, and from Java to eastern Germany, and that without the use of ships except along the Pacific coasts of Asia. At the height of Mongol power in the thirteenth century developments in one region were felt in others more quickly than at any time before the invention of modern communications. The organization which made this possible was an essential part of the Mongol achievement. The recruitment, the discipline, the strategy and tactics, the weapons and the equipment of the Mongol armies are subjects which need adequate treatment before the tale of conquest can be told. Some account is also needed of the social order and material culture of the Mongols. Much of the military and social fabric was inherited from the general tradition of nomadism on the eastern steppes of Asia, but decisive changes were made by the one Mongol leader of whom every reader will have heard: Chingis Khan.

The most obvious significance of the Mongols lies in their military achievement; their effect on the civilized peoples whom they overran, though terrific at their first impact, is less important. But for the general history of mankind on the largest scale their significance is somewhat wider. Though they were not the last of the nomad conquerors, theirs was the supreme attempt to impose nomad domination on the settled peoples of the world. In the long run the end of nomadism as a possible way of life for the rulers or even for any large proportion of mankind followed from its failure.

Since the Mongols campaigned and ruled in so many countries, the materials for a history of their doings are many and various. We have their own earlier traditions as written down during the second generation of their conquests. By the standards of modern scholarship an adequate history of the days of their greatness would require in the author not only a wide and detailed knowledge of history, ethnology and geography, but also a command of the original sources in Mongol, Chinese, Japanese, Burmese, Turkish, Persian, Armenian, Georgian, Syriac, Greek, Arabic, Russian, Latin, French and Italian in their medieval forms, such as no scholar can possess, though some have covered much of this range. The present short account naturally relies on translations and commentaries. Apart from written sources, archaeology and art provide some illumination.

Among Mongol sources, the purest tradition, that is, the most purely Mongol but not necessarily the most historical, is found in the *Secret History of the Mongols (Manghol-un ni'ucha tobcha'an)*, written down or compiled in 1240, perhaps by the Mongol Chief Justice Shigi Kutuku.[1] It is a mixture of myth, legend, and history, dealing with the ancestry and life of Chingis Khan, most of it before he led the Mongols against China. It is one of the very few contemporary accounts of a nomad people to come from within and not, like most accounts, from an external observer. Its title indicates that it was reserved for the reading of the royal house and of high officials only. A Chinese translation was prepared under the Ming Dynasty, the successor of the Yüan Dynasty of Mongols, in 1382, and is entitled *Yüan chao pi shi, Secret History of the Yüan Dynasty*, which is a little misleading because the material is earlier than the dynasty itself. The Mongol text was published only in the present century.

Another Mongol history, now vanished in its original form, was the *Altan Debter* or *Golden Roll*, of which the material was used by Chinese historians and by the Persian Rashid-ad-Din. Its relation to the *Secret History* is uncertain, but it appears to have been more of a chronicle or bare narrative and less of a literary, not to say poetical, work.[2] Later chronicles reaching down to the seventeenth century were added to the rest in the *Altan Tobchi* or *Golden Button*,[3] and in the *Mongol Khadun Toghuji* or *History of the Mongol Khans* by Prince Sanang Sechen, a devout Buddhist who adds edifying matter.[4] No Mongol text survives of the *Yasa (Law)*,[5] or of the *Bilik (Maxims)*[6] of Chingis, but there are still Mongol documents, such as inscriptions found in China, official documents and letters preserved in Iran, and the *yarlyks* or ordinances of the Khans in Russia.[7]

The main Chinese sources are: the official *Histories* of the later Sung Dynasty of South China and of the Chin Dynasty of North China, both overthrown by the Mongols; the official History of the Yüan or Mongol Dynasty itself; a few much earlier references in the Histories of the T'ang and Liao Dynasties, which knew of the Mongols as distant barbarians; and of course later accounts of the Mongols in the History of the Ming Dynasty, which turned them out of China. The regular *Histories* also contain sections of geographical and other information about foreign peoples and biographies of eminent persons, some of whom dealt with these peoples, particularly in war. There are also the personal writings of military commanders and travellers, and late compilations which preserve information from much earlier sources and finally merge with the beginnings of modern historiography in China. The Chinese *Histories* are basically annalistic and treat almost entirely of the Far East. They are written carefully and soberly in a uniform, impersonal and bureaucratic style.[8]

The Moslem historians, writing in Persian or Arabic or sometimes Turkish, have a very different background, for they are mostly not official historiographers. They have the Islamic belief in fate as the Will of God, but also a framework of general history, inherited ultimately from the Jews and the Christians, and remarkably amplified by knowledge arising from the Moslem conquests. A few of the most famous may be mentioned here.

Ibn-al-Athir of Mosul (1160–1233)[9] describes the Mongol conquest of Western Iran and Iraq from his own experience. Jakut-al-Hamawi, the geographer, tells of terror and ruin in Transoxania at the same time.[10] In 1241–42 Muhammad-al-Nasawi wrote a life of the adventurous Jelal-ad-Din, who was the last of the Khwarazmshahs and a valiant opponent of the Mongols.[11]

In Persian, 'Ala-ad-Din 'Ata Malik al Juvaini of Khurasan (1226–83), who spent his life in Mongol service, describes in his *Tarikh-i-Jahan Gusha* or *History of the World Conqueror*[12] the western conquests of Chingis and his successors in Central Asia and Iran down to those of Hülegü, founder of the Ilkhan Dynasty of Iran. Rashid-ad-Din Fadl' Allah (1247–1318), also an administrator, who served Ghazan Khan and his two successors, gives in his *Jami-at Tawarikh* or *Compendium of Histories*[13] a valuable account of the early history of the Mongols, for long the only one known in the west, and much more besides. This was commissioned by Ghazan Khan who wished to preserve his people's memory. Among other writers, who partly depend on these two, are the florid and prolix Ibn Fadl 'Allah of Shiraz, called Wassaf or the panegyrist,[14] who continued their account, and the compilers Abu 'Umar Menhaj-ad-Din al Juzjani[15] and Muhammad-ibn-Hawand Shah, usually called Mirkhond.[16] In Turkish, Abu'l Ghazi Bahadur Khan (1606–64), a descendant of Chingis and ruler of Transoxiana, wrote his *Shadjare-i-Türk* or *Genealogy of the Turks*,[17] which is in fact a history of the Mongols from Chingis onward.

In Syriac, Abu'l Faraj or Gregory Bar Hebraeus (b. 1226) wrote his *Maktebanut Zabul* or *Syrian Chronicle*, which adds details about Christians under Mongol rule.[18] The Nestorian patriarch Mar Yaballaha III (in office 1281–1317) is also a source for the Ilkhans.[19] In Armenia the chief contemporary sources are Gregory, of Akner in Cilicia or Little Armenia, author of a *History of the Nation of Archers*;[20] Hayton, or Hethum, of Armenia, who wrote in French *Le Flor des estoires de la Terre d'Orient*;[21] and the Armenian Marshal Sempad, who wrote a letter on his journey to Mongolia.[22] There are also the relevant parts of general histories of Armenia written by other natives.[23] Among Byzantine historians who treat of the Mongols are Georgios Akropolites in his *Chronike Syngraphe* on the years 1204–61, Georgios Pachymeres for the years 1255–1308, and Nikephoros Gregoras in his *Rhomaike Historia*.[24]

Russian, Polish and Lithuanian sources are not the writings of historians, but consist of chronicles and official documents from cities, courts and monasteries: treaties, laws, princes' wills, records of councils, official letters and the like. They are thus more difficult to use.[25]

In Catholic Europe, including Hungary, Moravia, Silesia and Germany, which were directly invaded, the documents are more easily intelligible to western readers because they are chronicles, letters and histories written against a familiar background. We have correspondence between Popes and Kings and the Great Khans and their officers. The *Speculum Historiale* of Vincent of Beauvais, the *Chronica Majora* of Matthew of Paris, the *Cronica* of Adam of Salimbene and the *Grande Chronique de la France* of Guillaume de Nangis are large works of the period containing references to Mongol operations in Europe and to the efforts of Popes and rulers to maintain discipline and courage.[26]

But the most revealing of western sources are the reports from friars, and later from merchants, of their own journeys in Mongol Asia, which represent the Mongols as seen by members of a third civilization besides the Chinese and Moslem. These are the *Itinerarium* and the *Historia Mongolorum* of John de Plano Carpini,[27] sent as a missionary by Innocent IV in 1245; the *Itinerarium ad Partes Orientales* of William of Rubruck,[28] sent in 1235 by Louis IX of France; and, as a pendant to Carpini's report, the *De Itinere ad Tartaros* of his companion Benedict,[29] and the newly discovered *Historia Tartarorum* written by another friar, C. de Bridia,[30] who used a manuscript by Benedict and conversations with him. These writers were Franciscans; the Dominican friars who were also sent to Mongol Asia have not left records of their own that survive, but much of their story is known.

After the death of Möngke Khan, when western Europe was no longer in danger of being overrun, the *Travels* of Marco Polo, called in its oldest manuscript the *Devisament dou Monde* or *Description of the World,* was written from Marco Polo's dictation in prison by his fellow prisoner Rusticiano.[31] This, the most famous of all the accounts of Mongol Asia, was written from the point of view of a practical merchant and traveller of very wide interests. Much less revealing is the *Relatio* of the Franciscan

Odoric of Pordenone,[32] who wandered begging through Asia in the same period.

The accounts of other Mongol doings, particularly those ordered by Kubilai in Japan and South East Asia, which are given in local sources, are of no more than marginal interest.

Something is added by archaeology in such places as the Crimea; the sites of Sarai, Old and New, the capitals of the Golden Horde on the Volga; and that of Karakorum in Mongolia. Sites in populous and settled countries such as China and Iran do not yield much that is distinctively Mongol, but in China at least there are inscriptions giving details of the lives of Mongol grandees. There is a considerable variety of Mongol coins found in different parts of Asia. Chinese, and in a greater degree Persian art, and Indian art in the Persian tradition, give authentic details of Mongol panoply and clothing and of Mongol life in court and camp. Here and there we find representations from Europe and Japan.[33]

CHAPTER I

The Mongols and the Nomad Tradition

THE COUNTRY NOW KNOWN as Mongolia had been the home of nomads for centuries before the Mongols became famous. It forms a distinct region of the northern steppes that extend from Hungary to Manchuria south of the northern forests. On its southern edge it has neither the inland seas nor the great mountains that border much of the steppes farther west, but the great cultivated area of China, apart from the Ordos Desert beyond the middle course of the Huang Ho. Between the Great Khingan Mountains on the east, which separate it from Manchuria, and the Altai and T'ien Shan ranges with interspersed deserts on the west, it is divided from north to south into three parts.

The northern part, which touches the Sayan and Altai and other ranges by Lake Baikal, consists of forested mountain and fertile prairie with many rivers and large lakes belonging to the systems of the Selenga, which flows into Lake Baikal, and of the Shilka and the Kerulen-Argun, which join to form the Amur. The central part comprises the Gobi Desert, 700 miles from north to south and 1,200 from east to west. The southern part is again grassland, traversed by two groups of low ranges north of the Huang Ho, of which the southern range carries the Great Wall of China. Western Mongolia is more desert than eastern, where there is pasture running southward by the Khingan. The whole country is a high plateau, mostly more than 3,000 feet above sea-level. The climate, except in the far north, is exceedingly dry and shows greater variation between summer heat and winter cold than in any other part of the steppes.

The climate of this and other parts of north-east Asia is thought to have produced over many thousands of years the so-called mongoloid physique which is now found here and also over much greater regions. The most marked feature is the skin, which is thick enough to show its inherent yellow colour, has fewer pores, hair-follicles and sweat-glands than in other races, and covers nerve-endings more deeply, so that heat and moisture are less easily lost by the body and cold is less felt. But the population has never been exclusively of this specialized physique; at all times there has been some admixture of the white races possessing a more abundant and a different growth of hair.

Though the physical difference between north Chinese and Mongols is not extreme, there have long been great differences of culture. One indication of this is language, for the Chinese language is quite unrelated to the Altaic group, which includes Mongol. The Altaic languages are likely to have arisen far to the north-west of the lower Huang Ho valley, the original seat of Chinese, and to have been spoken first by tribes who were still hunters in the northern forests. They are divided into three main groups, Turkish, Mongol, and Tungus, in that order from west to east. This sequence is still found where these peoples have remained in the forests or near them, but on the open steppe it has been continually altered by migration or conquest.

To the difference in language corresponds the difference between nomads and cultivators, which appears constantly in Chinese accounts of the Mongols and in the Mongol attitude to the Chinese and other settled peoples. The history of nomadism and particularly of mounted nomadism is of crucial importance for an understanding of the Mongols.

Nomadism on the northern steppes did not, as was once thought, arise directly from the primitive hunting economy by the capture and taming of sheep, cattle and horses that had once been common game. It is now argued that agriculture in these parts is older than nomadism; that when farming was introduced by slow spread from western Asia it already included both agriculture and stockbreeding. Within this mixed economy of domesticated animals and plants, stockbreeding would be so much more useful on light soils as to become dominant. Finally, specialists in stockbreeding abandoned agriculture altogether to follow and tend their browsing herds from one pasture to another. They kept such traditional skills as the making of tents and waggons and any form of metal-working that they knew, but their life and interests took on a completely different complexion from those of cultivators.

On the western steppes, where these developments took place during the third and second millennium B C, the nomads were white people who had once been farmers and had been influenced by the civilization of western Asia. Late in the second millennium the nomads took up riding as a regular habit, particularly for war, and in the centuries following 1000 B C spread themselves across the steppes as mounted conquerors whose favourite weapon was the bow. Some of them reached Zungaria and the Altai and the grasslands to the north and south of the Gobi. There they met mongoloid peoples, of whom those in the north at least had little or no contact with cultivators or civilized peoples. But most of the northern mongoloids were simply hunters and gatherers, and now passed directly from this mode of life to mounted nomadism and to fighting as cavalry. They became fiercer and tougher nomads than their white teachers.

By 400 B C, as Chinese records show, they had become formidable cavalry, who forced the Chinese to abandon the war chariot and to develop cavalry themselves. In the course of history the boundary in north China between cultivators and nomads grew sharper, so that during the last centuries B C the Chinese states began to build defensive walls mainly to hold back the nomads. As the Chinese states were gradually conquered and united by the strongest of them, Ch'in, so in the same period the nomads came to be organized in large groups of tribes, until finally the Chinese Han Dynasty, which succeeded the Ch'in late in the third century B C, found itself confronted by the nomad confederacy or empire of the Hiung-Nu under a line of paramount chiefs whose title was Shan Yü. The Hiung-Nu set a tradition in Mongolia which was followed closely by many nomad powers of later times, not least by the Mongols.

The Shan Yü had under him commanders or 'Wise Kings' of the Right and the Left, that is, of the western and eastern divisions of a southward-facing front, embodied not only in a battle-line but in a permanent grouping of tribes. These commands and other high offices were hereditary in three noble families. Each group of subject peoples ranged over a defined area for pasture. The army was organized in divisions of ten thousand horsemen, subdivided into thousands, hundreds and tens. It consisted of all free males of suitable age. In tactics much use was made of decoy troops who feigned flight in order to draw on a too confident enemy into ambush.

Chinese historians noted that in war-time the men of the Hiung-Nu practised riding and shooting, but in peace-time had nothing to do, while they themselves laboured in peace and were untrained for war. The nomads ate the flesh, drank the milk and wore the hides of tame animals without working for a living, and demanded from the Chinese tribute in grain and silk, and when there was not enough, trampled the crops under their horses' hoofs. When fathers died, their sons married their stepmothers of the polygamous household, and when brothers died, the remaining brothers married their widows. Every part of the description applies to the Mongols as the Chinese knew them a thousand or more years later, and many more similarities could be quoted.

The later empires of the Sien Pi, the Juan-Juan and the Turks followed the same pattern. From time to time parts of north China were ruled by such nomad peoples as the Hiung Nu, the Turkish Toba, the Mongol Khitans who founded the Liao Dynasty in 937, and the Tungus Juchens who superseded the Liao to found the Chin Dynasty in 1135. But none of these conquered the whole of China, as the Mongols finally did by the beginning of the fourteenth century, and after them the Manchus in the seventeenth. The greatest power before the Mongols to rule the steppes was the Turkish dominion in its various forms during the sixth and seventh centuries A D, which faced the great T'ang Dynasty on nearly equal terms but without prolonged warfare. The centre of Turkish power was usually north of the Gobi in the basin of the Orkhon, a tributary of the Selenga, the same region which the Mongols chose when they established their capital at Karakorum. It had the same decimal organization of the army, and its Khans regarded themselves as chosen by Heaven to rule all the nomads, as early inscriptions in the Orkhon valley show.

Much of the Mongol vocabulary of rule, of social organization, and of military command was taken from the Turks, for they once ruled the Mongols. Examples are: *ordu*, a great camp which was a headquarters or a court; *tümen,* 'ten thousand', particularly in the military sense of a cavalry division and its recruiting base; *khan*, for a paramount chief, and *khatun* for his wife or other great ladies; *darkhan* for a free man or later a minor chief; *ulus* for a people or group of peoples. Mongol history cannot be written without such words.

The Mongols were known to the Chinese for centuries before they became a menace. T'ang annals of the seventh century mention them under the name *Meng-wu* among a group of northern peoples called *Shi-wei*. The Meng-wu lived on the south bank of the river Shi-kien which flowed eastward from the lake Kui Lun; this must be the Argun, flowing out of Hulun Nor. The *Shi-wei* shaved their heads, used cattle to draw their carts, and lived in huts covered with mats or in tents transported on carts, like the Turks. Their saddles were of grass and their bridles of cord. They had few horses and no sheep, but many pigs and cattle. This is surely a description of tribes from the forests who were only beginning to live as nomads and were poor and ill-equipped. It is probable that others of the Shi-wei were Tunguses.

The *Meng-wu* or *Meng-ku* occur again in the Liao annals along with the *Ta-ta* or Tatars, as nomads, living on meat and sour milk, who raided China without much success. In the Chin annals they have become more dangerous. The second emperor, T'aitsung (1123–35), subdued a great part of Mongolia in the course of strengthening his dominion. The next emperor was reduced to defensive war or gifts. In raids the *Meng-ku* carried off Chinese and Khitan boys and girls and interbred with them. A further stage came when Kabul Khan of the Borjigin clan, an ancestor of Chingis, formed the great Mongol state *(Ta Meng-ku kuo)* bringing all the clans of the Mongols under his rule. At first he was a vassal of the Chin emperor, Hsi-tsung, but later went to war with him. When he eventually made peace and went to surrender at the Chin court, he was so mistrusted that a political representa- tive was sent to live at his camp. He had this officer murdered, so that war broke out again. The Chin used the Tatars against him. In the course of the war he died and was succeeded by his cousin Ambakhai. During a truce the Tatars treacherously seized Ambakhai and brought him with his cousin Okin Barkak as a prisoner to the Chin. The emperor had them put to death by nailing them to the wooden figure of an ass.

Under their next Khan, Kutula, the Mongols, with rebels from Manchuria, attacked the Chin again. A great expedition sent in 1143 was stopped by shortage of provisions and pursued and defeated by the Mongols. The Chin ceded forts which they held north of the Kerulen, but left troops in strategic positions. Later, Kutula, with four brothers, perished in a civil war, so that the power of the Mongols declined. They were again defeated in 1161 by the Chin and Tatars near Buyur Nor, and Chin suzerainty was restored over the whole region as far as the Kerait tribe in the west.

This was the situation about the time of the birth of Chingis. His father, Yesügei of the Borjigin clan, attempted to restore the power of the Mongols, but was poisoned by the Tatars before he had sufficient following to call himself Khan. He is always called simply *baghatur*, a title for a warrior, meaning 'champion' or 'hero'.

The Mongols proper, or Mangkhol, were one of a larger group of peoples who must be called the Mongol group to distinguish them from Turks and others. These peoples were divided into tribes and clans whose interrelations are not always clear. The Mangkhol and the Tatars were the further east, the former on the rivers Onon and Kerulen, the latter south of the rivers and about the Buyur Nor. Beyond their territories were the Khingan Mountains. Further south along the western slopes of the Khingan were the Khongirat; north of the Mangkhol and east of Lake Baikal were the Merkit and the Uriyankat; north of Baikal were the Buriyat and west of it the Oïrat and Tumet, forest-dwelling hunters rather than true nomads. West of the Mangkhol were the Kerait on the Orkhon and the Upper Selenga, and further west again the Naiman in forest and steppe. The Kerait and Naiman were much under Turkish influence, as titles and personal names show, and the chiefs at least were Nestorian Christians. South of the Gobi along the Great Wall were the Öngüt, also Nestorians, who were mixed Turks and Mongols. The Naiman, Kerait and Öngüt were the most advanced of these peoples, the Mongols in the east being much less so.

The basis of society in any Mongol people was the patrilinear clan or *obok*, which recognized as kin other clans descended from the same ancestor, so that intermarriage among such clans was forbidden. A group of kindred clans was called *yasun* (bone); clans of different *yasun* usually made a mutual arrange-ment for exogamous marriage. The *obok* itself was not entirely of one kin, for it contained beside the kin or *uruk* which controlled it, slaves and servants attached by defeat in war or other mis-fortune, who were known as *otole bogol* or *jalaghu*. Clans were grouped into a tribe known as *irgen* and tribes into an *ulus* or people or state. Entire clans or tribes with their chiefs, organization and grazing rights could be collectively subject to others. In this case they were called *unagan bogol*; ordinary members were serfs of their own chiefs and of the suzerain clan, but the ruling families intermarried with those of the suzerain. Defeated tribes could be added to the *unagan bogol*. Slaves and servants without organized kin were called *bogol* or *karachu*.

It was possible for chiefs to free members of the lowest class, who then received the title of *darkhan*, a mark of minor nobility; one privilege resulting was the holder's right to keep game that he had killed in the great battues organized by the Mongols as training in peace-time. Above the *darkhat* were nobles or *noyat*; the generals and many other officers of Mongol armies were called *noyan* (prince). Above these was the Khan, with his family. Outside the system of kinship two men might become *anda* or sworn brothers. Or again, a band of men might attach themselves as *nöküt* or personal followers to a noted chief. A *nökür* was more loyal and useful than any kinsman, especially to a rising chief who began as an isolated adventurer and needed followers of absolute devotion.[1]

Within the patriarchal order as described the position of women, in spite of their heavy tasks and the institution of polygamous marriage, was not so unfavourable. To be sure of a livelihood at all times of life it was necessary to belong to a family, and polygamy made this easier. Though there was concubinage, no distinction was made in legitimacy between sons of the same father by wives or concubines. Quarrelling among wives was rare. The practice by which the heir took over without marriage all his father's wives except his own mother shocked the Chinese and others, but it was very common among the Altaic nomads. It gave the widows and their children security against virtual enslavement and robbery of their goods and animals. In all matters but war and hunting the advice of women was continually sought, and in later times the widows of Khans served as regents. Mongol women were noted among other peoples for their loyalty and chastity.

The Mongols' mode of life[1] at this time was of the simplest nomad kind, except sometimes among the western tribes, which had most contact with such Central Asian Turks as the Uighurs, and among any others that had dealings with the Chinese. They kept cattle, sheep and goats, and increasingly large herds of horses on the Mongolian prairie. The horses were allowed to run half wild until the time came to break them in, when they would be caught by riders carrying nooses on the ends of long springy poles, a feat requiring much skill and strength. In the drier regions the Mongols were also beginning to use camels. Not all the tribes were yet committed entirely to the steppes; there were some who lived in forested territory. All of them remained skilful hunters, so that they could increase and vary their supply of food.

Their material culture is difficult to reconstruct from archaeo-logy, particularly for the earlier periods, because their remains were so perishable and comparatively little excavation has been done in Mongolia. Some features of modern Mongol equipment can be assumed for early times, but otherwise we are mainly dependent on the accounts of visitors from literate and non-nomad nations who reported what particularly struck them. There are also some indications to be found in such sources as the *Secret History*.

Plate 1

The food of the Mongols, as of other Altaic nomads, consisted chiefly of meat; that is, of mutton and more rarely of beef, supple-mented by the various kinds of wild game which they never ceased to hunt. It also included cheese and cheese-curd made from the milk of ewes, goats, cows and mares. Grain and rice, if they were eaten, would be imported. For drink they had milk and *kumiss*, the separated and fermented whey of mares' milk, which was both refreshing and warming, having an alcoholic content. Other drinks were imported by chiefs or the rich, among whom there was much drunkenness.

Their tents were, as now, circular structures of felt stretched over light wooden frames in a number of layers that varied according

Fig. 1

Fig. 1   Medieval Tartar huts and waggons (after Yule-Cordier)

to the season. Their shape was the best possible for standing firm in strong winds. The smaller tents could be unloaded from pack-animals or carts and set up in a very short time, and no less quickly taken down and loaded for transport. The larger ones were kept on special waggons and not dismantled. There were also two-wheeled carts with a chamber covered with felt for carrying valuables and especially small images of gods and spirits. The greased felt was proof against cold, wind and water; it could be painted white with lime or powdered bone, and in the door-flaps was usually adorned with paintings of birds, animals and trees. The frames were made in two parts. Below was a vertical wall-frame of trellis work, about five feet high, with an opening left for the entrance, enclosing a space twelve or fifteen feet in diameter. From the top of the wall a conical or domed roof frame of poles converged, like the spokes of an umbrella, on a small ring left uncovered to form a smoke-hole or ventilator. For short halts in suitable weather the roof alone would be set up. The covered carts and the waggons that carried the tents, especially the larger ones, were drawn by oxen, in later times as many as twenty, controlled by women.

Fig. 2

This round tent is now called a *ger*: the word *yurt*, commonly used for it by Russian and western writers, also meant in olden times 'homeland' or 'domain': so that Chingis Khan's *yurt* was Mongolia. It has been suggested that the round tent was not invented for use on the steppes but was originally a form of *tipi* or wigwam such as many tribes used in Northern Asia and North America, and that it was supplemented with a wall below to give more height and steadiness. The Mongols of today also have a low spreading tent, the *maikhan*, which requires much less wood and is used for caravans. This is likely to be at least as old as the developed *ger*.

From the accounts of medieval and modern travellers the interior arrangements and furnishing of the tent can be reconstructed with fair certainty for the thirteenth century. The round tents were set up to face southward, those of a group of related families forming a circle open to the south, with waggons drawn up round them for protection. Such a group was called an *ayil*. The interior of a tent was divided into two compartments. Visitors were admitted to the western compartment on their left; the eastern one was occupied by the women with their cooking utensils, large vessels of glazed earthenware for storing water and pails made from hollowed sections of tree trunk to hold milk and its products. In the centre of the tent was the hearth, directly under the smoke hole, equipped with a large trivet to receive the cauldron. Behind the hearth stood the master's raised couch on which he lay facing southward. To the left of this was a small square chest containing ornaments for clothes. Above the master's head hung an idol of felt called 'the master's brother': above his wife's another, 'the mistress's brother'. Another idol at the foot of the bed faced the servants at their work and one more on each side

Fig. 2 Drawing of Mongol ger, or yurt (after O. Lattimore, in 'Scientific American', August 1963)

watched over the women who milked the cows and the men who milked the mares. In the household of a Mongol of free status, to which our description applies, these would be serfs or thralls, living in their own tents near by. On goats' horns set in the wood-work were hung joints of meat, vessels, bows, and quivers full of arrows. The floor of the tent would be covered with felt, skins, or rugs laid on straw or dried grass. The gigantic tents of the Khans and their great officers would have been elaborations of this pattern.

Ordinary dress was as follows. Both sexes wore a long sack-like garment, opening from top to bottom and fastened over the breast, with trousers underneath. On their feet they wore boots of felt or leather. Cotton and silk were imported from China for the sum-mer versions of this dress, but even in summer woollen overcoats of similar pattern were worn in colder weather and felt capes against rain. The robe was folded double across the chest and fastened to the left with one band and to the right with three, the latter holding the outer fold. Women's dress was adorned with pleats and tucks and more modelled to fit the figure. Men wore leather belts on which quivers and bow-cases could be hung. Richer people's clothes had borders and piping of silk stuffed with wool. For warmth in the exceedingly cold winter, fur coats were worn, of varying quality according to the owner's means; an inner one with the hairs inside and an outer with the hairs outside. Fur caps were also part of the winter outfit. Women of rank wore a special headdress of bark or some other light material, over which was stretched a covering of silk: to this a bundle of feathers was fastened, rising into a plume like that of a helmet. Such was the celebrated *boktag* which drew the attention of travellers and is often shown in pictures. Ceremonial dress for Khans and dignitaries was an elaboration of these garments in richer silks and furs.

The labour expected of ordinary women was incessant. House-keeping included all the domestic trades required for nomad life: driving carts, setting up and dismantling the tents, milking cows, making butter, preparing skins and sewing them with sinew converted into thread, sewing footwear, socks and all other clothes, and making felt from wool for tents and clothing, as well as cooking and caring for the children. These clothes were not laundered and any attempt to do so, by daylight at least, was punished by other women with beating. Food vessels were never washed out with water.

The men made carts and waggons and the woodwork of tents; also bits, saddles of leather on wooden frames, and other harness, and of course bows and arrows and other weapons, and war and hunting equipment. They also kept and trained the horses and milked the mares. They beat mares' milk in great leather bags suspended from frames until the whey was separated from the curds for *kumiss*. Like the men, the women were expert riders, who sat astride and were trained to shoot with the bow. But the wealthier of them did so seldom; they were extremely fat, and crude in their use of cosmetics.

The burial of chiefs in imperial times is reported to have been very elaborate and many features of the ritual must have derived from much earlier times. But no burials have yet been found to confirm the accounts of Carpini, Rubruck or Marco Polo. Carpini even says that a Mongol grandee was buried sitting in his *yurt* with a table on which were a dish of meat and a jug of *kumiss*, and that a mare and foal and a horse with its saddle were buried with him, and that the skin of another horse, stuffed and impaled on a pole was set above ground. Though such descriptions recall many earlier styles of nomad burial, we are still unable to confirm their details from archaeology because the tombs of the Khans were hidden under replaced turf or replanted woodland with no mounds to mark them. Little is known of other burials.

The accounts at least show that the Mongols had a fixed belief in an afterworld where, like earlier nomad chiefs, theirs would need their horses and gear. They were also said to need servants and followers. There is little reason to doubt the report that all those who happened to meet the funeral processions of the great Khans on their way to the sacred mountain Burkhan Kaldun in Mongolia were slaughtered to serve their rulers beyond the grave. Such a custom is so like those of earlier nomads that the Mongols too may well have adopted it as soon as their chiefs became men of widespread power.

Mongol religion was of the type called shamanism, which was common among all the northern nomads and among other peoples of northern Asia. It lacked theology, dogma or philosophy, so that it was incomprehensible to Jews, Christians and Moslems, who had doctrines and scriptures. But it could be accommodated to the more superstitious forms of Christianity, such as Nestorianism as known in Central Asia, to which some medieval Mongols adhered, and to the cruder kinds of Buddhism, such as the later Mongols adopted almost universally. The shaman, or *kam* as the Mongols called him, was a wizard, prophet and medicine man, one of the earliest specialists that existed in any

33

activity. Among his other qualities he had the temperament and personality of a spiritualist medium, and acted as mediator between ordinary men, even rulers, and the world of spirits. The Mongols believed in an infinite number of spirits, some of them ancestral ghosts and others inhabiting and directing all the manifestations of nature in earth, water and sky including animals and vegetable life, on which their own lives depended.

Over all spirits reigned the great god of Heaven, Tengri, to whom the highest chiefs stood in a special relation as his particular servants. The will of Tengri, as well as of lesser spirits, was made known in oracles, dreams and visions, usually through the *kam,* but sometimes directly to the ruler. But although he decided awards and punishments even in this life, Tengri received very little cult from ordinary Mongols, though later under Chinese influence adoration and the burning of incense before a tablet inscribed with his name began to be practised. Nearer to daily life was the earth goddess Nachigai, otherwise known as Etügen of Itügen, mistress of grass, crops and herds, whose image was in every dwelling and received prayers for seasonable weather, for increase of crops and animals, and for the prosperity of the family.

The Mongols had a great number of religious observances and of superstitions, beliefs and rules which were little altered during the great conquests and survived until recent times. Prayers were offered to the idols of gods and spirits, the *ongot* which were made by the women from felt, silk or other stuffs, and of which some were kept in special waggons before the tents and in all military headquarters. Offerings of meat, drink and milk were smeared on their mouths at the beginning of meals and on other occasions. In later times a special *ongon* at each of the greatest headquarters represented the spirit of Chingis Khan. Obeisance to it was compulsory for all, Mongols or foreigners, on pain of death. The standard of Chingis also became a sacred object in which his soul was believed to dwell watching over his people. It received libations of *kumiss* thrown into the air. There were also horses dedicated to his spirit, which none dared ride. This cult of Chingis was an extreme example of the ancestor cult that was always part of Mongol religion.

Special reverence in the form of daily libations and obeisances was paid to the sun and the winds and to the points of the compass as habitations of spirits. Fire was considered a purifying element. The tent of a dead man and all his possessions were purified by being carried between two fires. This was particularly necessary if he had been killed by lightning. Foreign envoys likewise had to pass between two fires before receiving audience. No knife might be thrust into a fire, nor meat lifted with a knife from a cauldron resting on it or cut up near it. There were also other prohibitions, as on urinating in a tent or into running water, or even bathing in a stream, which must be obeyed on pain of death. These and many other tabus were of immemorial antiquity and protected the community from religious pollution. They had to be observed by Mongols and visitors to Mongol encampments.

Fig. 3 Chinese drawing of Chingis Khan. A conception rather than a portrait (after E. Huc, 'Souvenirs of a Journey through Tartary, Tibet and China', Vol. I)

CHAPTER II

Chingis Khan

THE RISE OF CHINGIS KHAN

THE EARLY LIFE of Chingis Khan, or Temujin as he was originally called, is given in picturesque and legendary detail in the *Secret History of the Mongols*. From the helpless position of one of Yesugei's orphaned and deserted family, Temujin rose rapidly by taking service with Toghrul Khan of the Kerait, the most powerful Mongol ruler of the time, who had been Yesugei's *anda* and who was honoured by the Chin with the Chinese title of *Wang*, or prince. The Wang Khan, as he is often called, was the chief vassal of the Chin among the nomads, and Temujin, through him, was likewise their vassal. At the *ordu* of Toghrul, or fighting his battles, Temujin met such famous warriors from various tribes as Jelme, Sübüdei, Jebe and Mukali, who were drawn by his remarkable personality to become his *nöküt* when many of his kin were his enemies.

Plate 2

The Mongols proper, who had begun to restore their fortunes, were eager to appoint themselves a Khan. There were many rivals for this position, including Jamuka, who had been Temujin's *anda* in boyhood, but had since quarrelled with him. Those of the Mongols who supported Temujin were at first less numerous and in bloody battles Jamuka's followers more than held their own, so that Temujin was forced to continue in Toghrul's service. But Jamuka did not create a power independent of Toghrul, for he too appears in his service from time to time. Gradually Toghrul became less friendly towards Temujin, though never to the point of hating him, as did his son Sengüm and Jamuka. Eventually, by a show of changing his mind and by issuing a false invitation, he tried to entrap Temujin; he, however, was warned and escaped death. It was now open war between Temujin and the Wang Khan.

In the first battle, at Kalakaljit-elet on the edge of the open steppe near the source of the Khalka in eastern Mongolia with Jamuka commanding the Kerait, Temujin's force fought successfully until the Kerait broke off the engagement when Sengüm was wounded in the cheek. But Temujin's numbers were not enough for further fighting and his losses were more serious than the enemy's, because harder to replace. He withdrew into the forests of the Khingan whither the Kerait neglected to pursue him, and gradually made his way to Lake Baljuna, north of the Onon, where his men already had their women and children.

Temujin waited there during the summer with his most loyal followers, among whom it became an honour to have drunk the bitter waters of Baljuna. He was joined by his brother Khasar, who had left his family and the Wang Khan. He used this circumstance to send two of Khasar's servants nominally to ask the Wang Khan to take Khasar back, but really to discover whether he was ready for battle. Guided by the returned spies

Fig. 3

and reinforced by new allies, he led his troops for a day and a night from a new position on the upper Kerulen to points where they could surround the Kerait in their camp at Jejer-ündür, apparently south of the Orkhon. They then attacked their un- prepared enemy for three days and nights of unceasing slaughter until they surrendered. The Wang Khan and Sengüm escaped, but later perished as refugees.

The battle of Jejer-ündür was the critical point in Temujin's conquests of Mongolia. After it, he campaigned against the Merkit and the Naiman, who were helped by Jamuka, until he had killed or driven out their Khans and princes and destroyed their states. In 1206 he was proclaimed the Chingis Khan or

Plates 3, 4

'universal ruler' of the *Yeke Mongol ulus*, which he now re- constituted at a *kuriltai*, or general assembly of chieftains. This is an important date in the history of the world: decisions taken then

Fig. 4

were to determine the fate of many peoples throughout Asia.

Fig. 4 Chinese drawing of Chingis Khan at some early stage consulting the 'lot-casters'. The oracular rods (tolga) were cast on the ground by a special diviner (tolgachin). They revealed by their manner of falling the future, or the likely consequences of actions (after P. Poucha)

Chingis set up his famous *tuk* or standard, like those of the Turkish Khans. It was a pole surmounted by nine white yak's tails that hung down from its head, nine being a sacred number. This was always carried in war when the Great Khan was in the field, while other commanders had less elaborate standards. After his death it was believed that his soul had entered the *tuk* and become identical with the *sulde* or guardian spirit of the Borjigin, protector of Mongol troops.

The shaman Kokchü announced that the Everlasting Blue Sky, Möngke Kökö Tengri, had made Chingis his representative on earth. The Borjigin clan became the *altan uruk*, the Golden Kin, ruling over a hierarchy of vassals. All its subjects of that day were called Mongols.

THE NEW MONGOL STATE AND ARMY

Chingis now organized his enlarged Mongol state on feudal lines under himself and his kin. Tribal arrangements were abolished, except where they accidentally fitted the new order, which was based on the decimal organization of the army as a permanent system both for peace and for war. The *Secret History* gives a long list of commanders of tens of thousands and of thousands, appointed from those who had served him faithfully.

Each of these commanders, the *noyan* or *beki* who led a group in war, was now the immediate ruler in peace of his men and their families. The term *noyan* did not denote a military rank, but was the general title of a feudal lord, alike of a *tümen* of ten thousand, a *mingan* of one thousand, a *jegun* of one hundred, or an *arban* of ten. A man was permanently under the orders of his *noyan*, and a lower *noyan* under a higher *noyan*. To leave one *noyan* for another was a crime punished by death.

Though the army was his first concern, Chingis is remembered no less for his *yasa* or system of laws for the Mongols, which was a codification of existing practice with additions of his own. The

Great Yasa was regarded by generations of Mongols in all parts of Asia as a magical document and a talisman of victory. It was written down by scribes in the Mongol form of the Uighur alphabet, though Chingis himself never learned to read. It bound in a like manner all members of the Golden Kin, for whom there were also special regulations. It apparently included regulations for the army. No text of its exists, but fragments are known from various sources.

The *Yasa* contained moral precepts: to honour the righteous and the innocent; to respect learned and wise men of every people; to love one another; to share food that was being eaten; not to steal; not to commit adultery; not to bear false witness; not to betray anyone; to spare the aged and the poor; to honour all religions and give preference to none. Except where foreigners are specifically mentioned, it is to be assumed from later descriptions of Mongol ways that these moral rules governed only the conduct of Mongols among themselves.

There were also rules which may be classified under inter-national law, at least by the end of Chingis's reign. It was assumed that the Great Khan was commissioned by God to conquer and rule the earth, so that resistance to any Mongol demand for submission was rebellion against God. If foreign peoples submitted, they would be well treated, but if they resisted, the formula was: 'As for us, what do we know? The Everlasting God knows what will happen to you.' The existence of sovereign states equal with the Mongol Empire was not admitted. This doctrine was used to justify any atrocity, in conquest as in pacifica-tion. The personal touch of Chingis can be clearly seen.

The foundation of the Great Khan's power was the statute of bound service, which laid it down that no man could desert any position in which he was placed or any work which he was set to do. The burden was equally distributed without regard to wealth or standing. The *Yasa* provided the necessary powers for taxation, conscription and the courier service, and bound all able-bodied Mongols to take part in the great hunt for game which was conducted in winter, partly to add to the supply of meat, but more importantly as a military manoeuvre under the Khan's eye and subject to his final review of performance. But priests of all religions, physicians and scholars were exempted from regular duties and taxes.

Criminal law punished the usual offences against person, property, marriage, public order and the course of justice, usually with death, which was also the penalty for gluttony. The death sentence was also imposed for serious offences against military discipline and efficiency; for such acts as charity to captives without consent of their captor, or withholding a runaway slave or prisoner from recapture; for being in possession of a stolen horse without being able to pay the fine; for stepping on the threshold of a military chief's tent, or, if a high officer, for asking favours of anyone but the Khan. It was also the punishment for commercial fraud and bankruptcy, and for specifically religious or ritual offences such as killing animals in the Moham-medan manner in violation of Mongol rite, bathing in running water, or urinating into water or ashes or inside a tent. Less serious offences were punished with heavy fines or beating with stout sticks. Persons of royal rank were put to death without bloodshed by clubbing and pounding inside a rug or carpet.

The army as constituted in 1206 was still organized in *tümens* as described, but was dominated henceforward by the greatly augmented Imperial guard, the *keshik*, which was an inheritance from the Turkish Khans and from such Mongol Khans as Toghrul. But under Chingis it took on a special character.

The original lifeguard of the Khan was increased from 1000 to 7000, each man being now a *baghatur*. The day-guard *(turga'ut)*, the night-guard *(kebte'ut)* and the quiver-bearers *(korchi)* were all raised to 1000. Members of the Guard were also grooms and cooks and doorkeepers. The entire *keshik* now numbered more than 10,000 with its officers. It was the crack force of the entire

*Fig. 5 Chinese drawing of Mongol war-
rior in scale armour with heavy curved
sword, bow, arrows and spear slung
behind him (after E. Huc)*

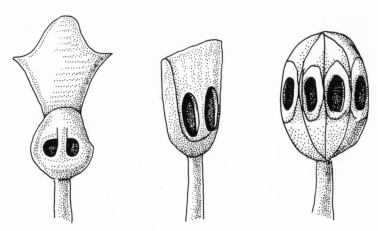

Fig. 6   Whistling arrow-heads through which the air passed as they flew. By their sound they gave the signal for other arrows to be shot after them at the same target. They could be used for other signals too (after W. Heissig)

army, recruited from the whole Mongol people by a process of sifting, for every unit was represented by sons of its commander and others specially chosen. Through it, Chingis was in touch with all the people. A private of the *keshik* was thought fit to command any unit of other troops at need. The *keshik* also served as the Military Academy and Staff College, for the highest appointments were kept for its members. In the field it was placed in the centre with the Khan when he was with the army, and it was used to decide the issue of a battle. Its members were always on active service, for this included attendance on the Khan, wherever he might be.

Discipline in the army was severe and practical. Officers had to inspect the weapons and equipment of their men before battle and to supply all deficiencies on pain of punishment after the Khan's inspection. If any man dropped anything in battle the man riding behind him must return it to him. Plundering without permission, deserting a comrade in the *arban* and sleeping on guard

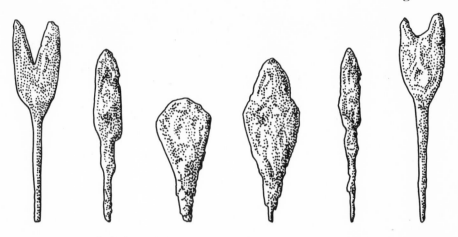

Fig. 7   Iron arrow-heads from Karakorum. Those at either end, with crescent heads, are approx. 11 cm. long and intended for slicing flesh; the rest, drawn in proportion, are for piercing it in the usual way (after Kiselev, 'Drevnemongolskie Goroda')

were punished with death. Officers who did not attend the Khan's addresses or who failed to control men on campaign were removed. A man who was physically very much tougher than other men must not be put in command, because he could not feel hunger and thirst as they did and would thus reduce their efficiency. The Mongols thus became not only a warlike but a military nation.

Weapons and armour were of well-known nomad patterns, with some additions. Each trooper possessed a short compound bow made of various pieces of springy wood fastened firmly round a central core and another longer bow of the same kind for fighting on foot, both with a range of more than 200 yards; and arrows, light for long range, and heavier, with broad heads, for close range, thirty of each kind in separate quivers; also a sword and a light sharp sabre and, if in the heavy cavalry, a lance. Armour consisted of conical steel caps with leather neck-pieces, jerkins of hide lacquered against damp, in later times often

Figs. 6, 7, 11

Figs. 8, 9
Figs. 5, 10

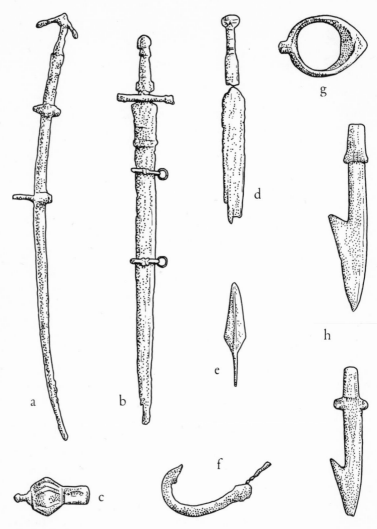

Fig. 8   Weapons and gear from the territory of the Golden Horde ; a and b, sabre and sword of uncertain provenance ; c, iron spear-butt ; d, bone sword-hilt ; e, arrow-head ; f, iron fish-hook ; g, bronze ring for stringing bows ; h, bone harpoons (after Yakubovski)

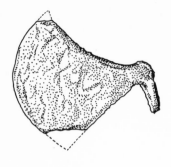

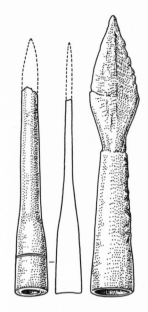

Fig. 9 Iron weapons from Karakorum. Above: head of a socketed battle-axe (width of blade 16.5 cm.). The tubular socket is cracked and worn. Right: two spear-heads (after Kiselev)

covered with overlapping scales or strips of metal, and shields of skin or willow-wood in four sizes according to their purpose. Shields would not have been used by men fighting as mounted archers, but would be required with swords and sabres.

The Mongols rode ponies thirteen or fourteen hands high, which were watered once a day and mostly fed on growing grass. These were not ridden at all until they were three years old, and then, if possible, for one day only with three or four days' rest, during which time remounts were ridden instead. Sometimes as many as twenty remounts followed each rider. These horses could be assembled easily in herds of 10,000 on the rich pastures of northern Mongolia, and never strayed.

Equipment consisted of a hatchet, a file for sharpening arrows, an awl, a fish-hook and line, a tow-rope, an iron cooking-pot, two leather bottles, one for water, the other for *kumiss*, a water-proof leather kit-bag, a fur helmet and sheep-skin coat for

*Fig. 10   Miniature from a manu-
script of Rashid-ad-Din (probably the Edinburgh MS.) showing
a Mongol warrior in lamellar
armour that covers him from the
neck down to the elbow and
lower leg (after Russell Robinson,
'Oriental Armour')*

extreme cold, and to every so many troopers a tent and a light
circular hide fitted with loops round the edge to take a cord, which
served as a ground-sheet. Rations were of dried meat and cheese
from mares' milk, but the troops were expected to live by foraging
and hunting. In later times a soldier had also a waggon to carry
spare weapons and three slaves.

Fig. 11   Japanese pictures of Mongol archers from the Mongol Invasion Scroll (after Russell Robinson)

An army moved in columns, usually at some distance apart but kept in touch by fast-riding messengers. It could be quickly divided for simultaneous thrusts in different directions or for converging from several points of the compass on one objective. This power of dispersion was useful in crossing arid country and also served to magnify the apparent number of invaders. Camels

Fig. 12 *Chinese and Saracen siege-engines as used by the Mongols: ballistae for throwing heavy stones and other massive missiles (after Yule-Cordier)*

Fig. 12

Fig. 13

Plate 20

Plate 25

were later added in great numbers for transport, and siege-engines and gun-powder, and techniques of mining and sapping, were taken over from the Chinese. Signalling was done by flags during the day and by torches at night; the assault was announced by kettle-drum and trumpet, and sometimes by the playing of a short piece of music.

The attack was begun by the *kara'ul* or light-armed vanguard, followed by an advance of quick-shooting archers, who then retired to allow the heavy cavalry to pass through them. The advance was usually made in silence, the main body moving forward in close formation and at the steady pace called the 'wolf-lope'. Constant use was made of feigned flight and ambush, and pursuit was always ruthless.

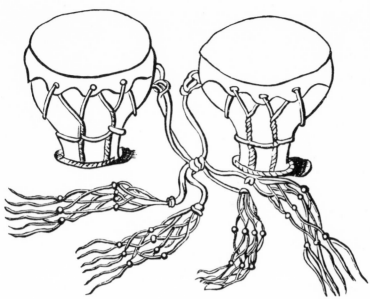

Fig. 13   Chinese drawing of nakkaras or kettle-drums of bronze and hide. The smallest, approx. 1 m. in diameter, were probably carried on camels ; the largest, approx. 2.5 m. across, were carried on elephants in Kubilai's wars (after Yule-Cordier)

THE FIRST FOREIGN CAMPAIGNS

Order having been established in Mongolia, Chingis, with an army of twelve *tümens*, was ready for foreign adventures. He was eager to destroy the Chin, who had put to death illustrious members of his clan. But first he needed to secure his rear against other nomads and to encircle the Chin on their northern borders.

Plate 8

In 1207 Chingis sent his eldest son Jöchi with the Army of the Right, or West, against the Oirat and Buriyat and against the Turkish Kirghiz on the Yenisei, and also against the Tumet. These were all subjugated and presented to Jöchi as his appanage, a foretaste of his great dominion in the west.

Fig. 14

To the south lay the kingdom of Si-Hia in the Ordos desert and in Kansu with great mountains beyond it. It would be a threat

51

from the west to any invader of China. It had been founded by the Tangut nomads from Tibet after the fall of the T'ang, and was a stronghold of Buddhism and of Chinese culture. Its army of 150,000, part cavalry, part infantry, was trained on Chinese lines.

Chingis, who had already raided this territory, now crossed mountain and desert to Urahai, and defeated an army of 50,000 sent to stop him. When they advanced on the capital, Chungsing or Erikaya, beyond the Ala-Shan, the Mongols were held up for two months by another army of 50,000 under the Tibetan Ashagambu, until Chingis by pretending flight drew the enemy down from their position and cut them to pieces in an ambush. He then besieged the capital, which was protected by a system of irrigation-canals filled from the Huang Ho. A dyke was built downstream to hold back the river, which then flowed into the city with great destruction. The king, Li An-chüan, received no help from the Chin emperor, who said that the Tangut were disloyal vassals. The siege lasted until 1210, when the dyke burst. The Mongols had to retire, but the Tangut submitted and Ashagambu was made prisoner.

Further west, Chingis turned his attention to the kingdom of Karakhitai, ruled by the Si-Liao, or western Liao, a remnant of the Chinese Liao, who had been led westward in 1129 by Ye-liu Tai-shi of the Khitan royal clan when the Liao fell in China. The capital was at Balasaghun on the Chu, and the territory covered Zungaria, the Tarim basin and Transoxiana, The Khitan rulers used the Turkish title Gurkhan because most of their subjects were Turks, but maintained Chinese culture and a form of Buddhism at court. Karakhitai was now in full decline and vassal rulers were exasperated by heavy taxation. In 1209 Barchuk, the Idikut or sacred ruler of the Uighur Turks at Bishbalik, rose against the Gurkhan and attached himself to Chingis. Chingis accepted his suit and sent an army right through his territory to the valley of the Ili where Arslan, Khan of the Karluk Turks and Buzar, king of Almalik, readily became his

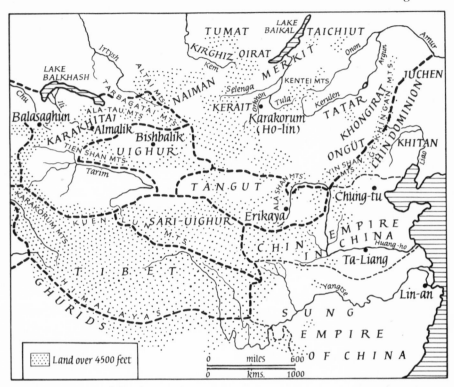

Fig. 14   Eastern Asia before the Mongol expansion

vassals. Perhaps the most important result was that literate
Uighur officials began to take service under the Mongol state.

THE CAMPAIGN IN CHINA

Now that he had learned to campaign across the driest desert and
had captured a good supply of camels, Chingis decided to strike
directly across the Gobi against the north of China.

His enemies, the Chin, had an army estimated at five hundred
thousand, of whom one hundred and twenty thousand were

mounted bowmen of nomad Juchen origin. Their defensive system consisted of the Great Wall and also of two lesser walls, one running southward along the Khingan to meet it, the other continuing it westward to the border of Si-Hia, through the territory of the Öngüt, whose chief was friendly to Chingis. East of the Khingan and also along the westward-running wall were the grazing grounds of the Chin cavalry. The capital, Chung-tu, on the site of modern Peking, was further protected by an inner wall along mountains to the sea, and by fortified passes.

In 1209 Chingis rejected with contempt an embassy sent by the emperor Wei Shao Wang to collect tribute, and proceeded to build up his forces, using spies, neutral merchants and dis-affected Chinese officials to gather intelligence. Leaving a force of twenty thousand under his youngest brother, Temüge, to guard Mongolia, he moved his forces in 1211, probably by three routes, across the Gobi. The Army of the Right, perhaps forty thousand strong, under the princes Jaghatai, Jöchi and Ögödei, aimed at Ching Chou. To the east the Armies of the Centre and Left, under Chingis and his officers, made the main advance towards Huan chou, north of Chung-tu, and further west towards Ta shi luan. Having crossed the desert before the heat of summer, making good use of their camels for transport, the Mongols were by May among the good pastures of the Öngüt country within striking distance of the Ye-hu-ling range which protected the plain of Chung-tu.

The Chin concentrated their troops to face these eastern armies. On the direct route to the capital, the pass leading from Huan-er-tsi to the Yang valley, Wan-yen Hu-sha was ordered to fortify Wu-sha-pao while two hundred thousand men under Ke-shi-lie Chih-chung were to build defences along the Ye-hu-ling. Guided by the Khitan Ye-liu Tukha, Jebe by a round-about route fell upon Hu-sha's force and destroyed its work. Chih-chung's plans were betrayed to the Mongols by another Khitan, Shih-mo

Ming/an, who had been sent to parley. When his assembled army attacked at Huan/er/tsi, its cavalry, placed too close in front of its infantry, was driven back in confusion by the arrows of the Mongol light horse and by the charge of the heavy cavalry under Mukali and of the *Keshik* under Chingis. The Chin infantry were thus thrown into confusion. Their whole army, now broken, fled through the pass, and was cut down in a pursuit that covered thirty miles. Meanwhile, the western army of the Mongols took towns on the Huang Ho and captured many horses.

Jebe then captured the great Chü Yung Kuan fortress, which blocked the main pass leading to Chung/tu, drawing out its defenders by a feigned flight into a disastrous battle. Chingis now occupied Lung/hu/tai, less than twenty/five miles from Chung/tu, and plundered the plain. Jebe failed to take the capital by assault, but did capture the eastern capital, Tung/ching, by the same ruse of feigned flight.

In Spring 1212 the Mongols withdrew to the Öngüt country. But they returned in autumn to destroy another Chin army under Ao Tun/hiang, which they trapped in a valley as it advanced to relieve the town of Hi/ching. But Chingis was wounded in the assault and they retired northward. The Chin reoccupied the fallen town of Te/hing/chou. In 1213 the Chin, in spite of famine, Chinese insurrection, Khitan rebellion and Tangut attack, sent a new army of a hundred thousand to Wei/chuan, north of the Chü Yung Kuan. This, too, Chingis annihilated by a frontal assault with his centre while his wings, passing along the neighbouring heights, drove in the Chin flank and rear. Though the Chin army was destroyed, the reoccupied Chü Yung Kuan would not surrender. But Jebe, advancing by other valleys, took by surprise the other great fort, the Tzu Ching Kuan. The Mongols then surprised the Chü Yung Kuan from the south. But when Chingis offered terms to the Chin, they refused.

Inside Chung/tu, the emperor Wei Shao Wang was executed by Chih/chung, who replaced him with Huan/tsung, but was himself murdered, while three Chinese generals went over to the Mongols. Though Huan-tsung tried to make peace, Chingis began systematically to devastate north China with three armies whose advances divided from one another the remnants of the Chin forces. One drove through western Hopei and Shansi, one between Chung-tu and the sea, and the third through eastern Hopei and Shantung. Regimented captives were driven forward to erect siege engines under shot and to be slaughtered by the defenders as they headed assaults. But Chingis held only the fortified passes and the towns about Chung-tu.

The Mongols were still unable to take Chung-tu by assault. The city had walls of stamped clay 40 feet high with battlements of brick, nine hundred towers, twelve or thirteen gates and three moats. Connected with it by subterranean tunnels were four smaller cities, each about a mile square and equipped with its own arsenals and stores. The main city was defended by twenty thousand soldiers and each of the outer cities by four thousand, who could take attackers in the rear.

Chingis now again proposed terms, which were finally accepted in May, when Huan-tsung handed over a daughter of Wei Shao Wang with girls and boys, horses, gold and silk. But when the Mongols had gone, the emperor decided, against his Ministers' advice, to move to the southern capital Ta-liang. This was a desertion of the northern provinces and of the Juchen homeland in Manchuria. It was also taken by Chingis as a sign of mistrust and a breach of the treaty. The Mongols prepared to march southward again.

Plate 9

In 1215 the Mongol Samukha laid siege to Chung-tu with a force of 50,000 Mongols, Khitan and Chinese. Food and reinforcements sent northward from Ta-liang were cut off, and the entire Mongol army under Mukali now besieged Chung-tu. Under stress of hunger the gates of Chung-tu were opened to Shih-mo Ming-an, who was now in command of siege-works. The besiegers sacked much of the city and killed thousands of the inhabitants. Heaps of bones and rotting corpses astonished an embassy from Khwarazm that passed that way. A gigantic booty was forwarded to Chingis, along with high officials, one of whom, Ye-liu Chu-tsai, of the Khitan royal clan, so impressed Chingis with his dignity and loyalty to his former masters that he at once took him into his service, with important consequences for China.

The Chin had lost authority north of the Huang Ho, and faced famine and peasant revolt south of it, but they defeated a Tangut invasion, raised a new army, garrisoned forts round Ta-liang, and manned the great fortress of Tung Kuan to bar advance down the Huang Ho.

Under various generals, Mongol armies again overran the province north of the Huang Ho, and an armistice was now offered to Huan-tsang, if he would accept the minor title of King of Honan, the province just south of the river. But he still refused. The Mongols next destroyed the Chin dominion in Manchuria and reduced Korea to tribute. In 1217 Mukali was appointed by Chingis to carry on the war with full powers, symbolized by the title *Go ong*, Prince of State, and the right to set up a nine-tailed *tuk*. Chingis had been drawn into another great war and never saw China again.

THE WAR AGAINST THE KHWARAZMSHAHS

Chingis had returned to Mongolia in 1216 to safeguard northern Mongolia and his conquests in Karakhitai. Güchlük, the son of the Naiman Tayang Khan, had taken refuge in 1208 with Chiluku, the Gurkhan, and married his daughter. In 1211 he had deposed Chiluku and taken the central part of his kingdom, leaving the western part to be occupied by Muhammad the Khwarazmshah. He became a Buddhist to please his wife and persecuted his Moslem subjects. He aimed at conquering the whole of Karakhitai and fought with some success against the

Khwarazmshah. To check his eastern ambitions, Chingis in 1217 sent Jebe with twenty thousand Mongols against him. After skilfully winning over the Moslems with a policy of toleration, Jebe pursued Güchlük into the mountains of Badakhshan until he was caught and beheaded. The Mongol Empire now reached the Pamir and the Syr Darya, where it bordered Khwarazm.

Meanwhile in Mongolia Chingis reorganized the administration of his territories, relying greatly on the advice of Yeliu Chutsai. When the Mongol generals proposed to exterminate most of the northern Chinese and to use their land for grazing, Yeliu Chutsai saved their lives, not by making any plea of humanity but by showing how the Mongol state could benefit by taxes on land, commerce and the production of salt and iron. Chingis gave him authority to carry out his schemes; for a beginning the poll tax was made universal. A central chancellery was formed under Yeliu Chutsai, for which Chinese, Uighurs and, later, Central Asian Moslems were recruited.

Fig. 15

During these years the power of the Turkish Khwarazmshahs had grown up to the west of Karakhitai. It was founded by Atziz, who died in 1156, and by his successor Takash, who drove his former masters, the Seljuks, from Central Asia, dominated the Karakhanid princes of Transoxiana and seized Khurasan. But Takash did not try to destroy his other suzerains, the rulers of Karakhitai, whom he regarded as a bulwark against the eastern nomads. His son Muhammad was less prudent; he saw himself as 'the swordarm of Islam'.

Muhammad, who succeeded in 1200, watched with pleasure while Güchlük overthrew the Gurkhan, but later fought against him as a persecutor of Moslems. In the far north, where he was campaigning with an army of sixty thousand, Muhammad encountered a force of twenty thousand Mongols under Sübüdei, who had been sent to destroy a remnant of the Merkit. He attacked these infidels too, but the battle was no more than a draw, and had no immediate consequences.

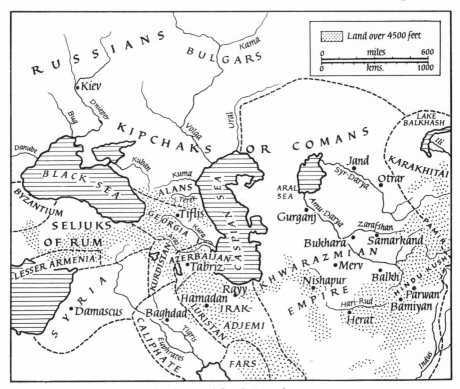

Fig. 15 Central and western Asia and Russia before the Mongol conquests

Muhammad extended his empire over much of Afghanistan and part of northern India. He also tried to coerce his religious superior, the Caliph Nasir of Baghdad, desiring to destroy his temporal power. This enmity was a source of weakness for the Khwarazmian Empire and for the whole of Islam in Asia. His power was also weakened by a standing feud with his formidable mother, the Kipchak princess Turkhan Khatun, and with the Karakhanids who favoured her. His Iranian officials were everywhere on bad terms with his Turkish commanders and troops and hated by the peasants whom they taxed.

The first exchanges between Muhammad and Chingis were friendly. In 1215 Muhammad's embassy, which saw the devastation round Chung-tu, was graciously received by Chingis, who said that the rulers of the west and of the east should be at peace and should promote trade between their empires.

In 1218 Chingis sent an embassy offering Muhammad a treaty of peace and the status of 'dearest of his sons'. Muhammad made the treaty, but was piqued by the suggestion of vassaldom. Soon after the embassy, a caravan came westward under four Moslem merchants with four hundred and fifty men and five hundred richly loaded camels. On arriving at Utrar on the Syr Darya, they were detained by the governor, Inalchik, arrested, robbed of their merchandise and put to death on the charge of spying. Whether or not Muhammad ordered this action, he certainly condoned it and shared in the plunder.

Chingis sent his ambassador Ibn Khafraj Bughra with two Mongols to demand that Inalchik be surrendered to punishment; otherwise the lives of Muhammad's subjects would have little value. He sent this ultimatum only after seeking guidance from Heaven, but Muhammad refused, put Bughra to death, and sent back the two Mongols with their beards shaved off.

Such violation of the persons of ambassadors could only be answered with war. Chingis summoned all Mongols between the ages of seventeen and sixty, and contingents from the Kip-chaks, the Karluks, the Uighurs, the Khitans, the Juchens and the Chinese. The Tangut king insultingly refused to cooperate, persuaded by Ashagambu, who had been released. Chingis resolved to destroy his kingdom even if it were his last act.

In the summer of 1219 Chingis mustered on the upper Irtysh an army of more than a hundred and fifty thousand, all cavalry except for some ten thousand siege-engineers from China, who were equipped with catapults, mangonels, ballistae for hurling heavy blocks of stone, primitive cannon charged with gunpowder that would fire balls of stone or iron, and flame throwers for close attack. Another Chinese invention was an undershirt of raw silk, which an arrow would not penetrate, but only drive into the wound so that the head could easily be pulled out. The heavy artillery was loaded in pieces onto yaks and camels. A road with timber bridges, wide enough to take two carts abreast, was driven through the Altai, and well guarded depots were set up there, and by advance parties in the desert, to hold supplies and animals for transport and for meat. Moslem interpreters familiar with the west were assigned to all divisions and intelligence was diligently collected.

Muhammad's forces numbered perhaps three hundred thousand, but he distrusted his generals too much to gather them in one place, and chose instead to leave in the most important cities large garrisons or even full armies, who might also act as a defence in depth, for example fifty thousand at Utrar and a hundred thousand at Samarkand. He himself retired to Balkh, hoping to raise further and more loyal troops. His plan of adding an outer wall fifty miles long to the oasis of Samarkand, for which three years' taxes were to be raised in one year, made no progress.

The Mongols, collecting their last allied contingents on the Kayalik Steppe south of Lake Balkash, crossed six hundred miles of desert to Utrar, which was still held by the guilty Inalchik. Chingis left there several *tümens* who after six months took the citadel and put Inalchik to death. Of the rest of the army, one part under Jöchi took the towns on the lower Syr Darya, while another force took the upper valley. Chingis himself pressed on across the Kizil Kum desert to take Bukhara. Most of the Turkish garrison cut their way out, but were later pursued and killed. The defenders of the citadel were massacred and the mass of the citizens driven out with no more than the clothes that they wore, while the cathedral mosque and the palace were plundered and most of the town was set on fire.

Chingis then marched down the Zarafshan to Samarkand which was held by a mixed force of Turks, Iranians and Afghans,

Plate 5

Plate 6

Plate 21

said to have numbered a hundred and ten thousand. On the third day of the siege a sortie of the inhabitants, more than fifty thousand strong, was ambushed and cut down; on the fifth day the garrison and all the rest surrendered. The *kadi* and the *shaykh* were left with fifty thousand persons under their protection, but the rest were driven out while the city was flooded from the canal and destroyed. Thirty thousand craftsmen were carried off as slaves and many more drafted for siege-work. The rest were allowed to return after paying an indemnity. The Mongols overcame all the other cities of Khwarazm by siege or surrender without ever meeting a Khwarazmian army in the field. The cities, which were built in oases and depended on irrigation and careful gardening, never entirely recovered. They lost for a long time their pre-eminence in every kind of Islamic learning, culture and art.

Three *tümens* were sent westward across the Amu Darya in pursuit of Muhammad, who fled before them from Balkh through city after city of northern Iran until he escaped to the island of Abakan, off the southern shore of the Caspian, where in 1220 he died of pleurisy, appointing Jelal-ad-Din to succeed him.

The last Khwarazmian city to fall was Gurganj on the Amu Darya, where Jelal-ad-Din stayed for a time before he was forced to flee from a conspiracy. It resisted obstinately a force of a hundred thousand under Jaghatai, Ögödei and Jöchi. When it fell, its people were massacred, except for a hundred thousand craftsmen, the children and the young women. Jöchi, who was to rule it, could not prevent this destruction.

By 1221 Jelal-ad-Din was in Ghaznah, south of the Hindu Kush, preparing further resistance. Chingis, advancing through very mountainous country to attack him, destroyed many towns, including the famous Buddhist centre of Bamiyan. Jelal-ad-Din actually won an important battle at Parwan with ninety thousand men against a Mongol force under Shigi Kutuku, but after his victory he was deserted by his Ghurs and Afghans, who quarrelled with his Turks. He fell back to the Indus with fifty thousand, and was eventually penned against the river below Peshawar. All his men were killed or driven into the river, but he escaped by leaping with his horse from a thirty-foot cliff into the current. He escaped into the Punjab, and was pursued without success. His stand brought about revolts in Herat, Merv and Balkh, which were taken by the Mongols after laborious sieges. One and a half million people are said to have been slaughtered at Merv, and Balkh is reported to have been deserted except for a few barking dogs. In 1223 Chingis set out homeward, having destroyed another empire and for the time ruined the power of Islam in Central Asia.

Plate 7

JEBE AND SÜBÜDEI IN CAUCASIA AND RUSSIA

The force sent in pursuit of Muhammad was commanded by Jebe and Sübüdei, who, after overrunning north-western Iran and taking Kasvin, wintered on the Steppe of Mughan in Azerbaijan. There they were attacked by ten thousand cavalry, sent by George IV, king of Armenia. They cut this force to pieces, and advanced up the Kura against Tiflis, where they defeated the main army of Georgia, but could not take the city. Returning to Iran, they took and plundered Hamadan and sent an embassy to Baghdad, demanding tribute from the Caliph. They then prepared to invade Russia, taking part, as we now know, in a joint attack with Jöchi, who was ordered to go westward from the Aral Steppe to meet them on the Volga, but did not do so because of illness.

Fig. 16

They passed through Georgia, defeating another army, and on through Shirvan and Derbend, dragging their waggons and siege-engines over bridged ravines. They defeated the Kipchak and the Alans and overran the Ukraine and the Crimea, where they spent the winter of 1222–23. In spring, they heard that Russian forces from various cities, eighty-two thousand strong, were gathering

Fig. 16   Chinese drawing of Sübüdei (after Iakoubovski and Grekov, 'La Horde d'or et la Russie')

to attack them under Mstislav of Galich, assisted by some tens of thousands of Kipchak cavalry. Mstislav's army crossed the Dniepr to attack them without waiting for another large force from the north and without the Kipchak cavalry. The Mongols tired the Russians with a long retreat to the Kalka, and gave battle on its banks. The Russian advance guard was driven back in confusion onto its main body, which was not ready. The whole army was destroyed, and so too was the second Russian force, which arrived without knowing the plans of the first. A third army, coming from Kiev, was besieged behind a palisade and driven in rout to the Dniepr. Jebe and Sübüdei were now recalled eastward. On their way they attacked Great Bulgaria on the Volga. Jebe died, but Jöchi joined in the attack. The Mongols determined to return to Russia in greater force with Jöchi to lead them.

THE TANGUT CAMPAIGN AND THE DEATH OF CHINGIS

Chingis now prepared to punish the Tangut. To meet him, Ashagambu mustered a large Tangut army with allies from Tibet and from the Chin. Like Muhammad in Khwarazm, he intended to keep his forces in strong walled cities, not in the open field.

In the spring of 1226 Chingis, now seventy-two years old, marched from the Kerulen with a hundred and fifty thousand men including Afghans and Ghurs. Though he had a bad fall from his horse and was taken ill with a fever, he continued on his way, and routed an army of Tibetans and Turks on the border of Si-Hia. His army then captured Erijayu, the second city of the kingdom. In September Chingis met Ashagambu's army in a flooded plain by the Huang Ho, which had become a sheet of ice. The Mongols, whose horses' hoofs were bound with cloth to prevent slipping, annihilated the Tangut army and pursued its remnants to the Ala Shan, where Ashagambu was caught.

Early in 1227 Jöchi died of an illness. Chingis ordered Temüge to instal his son Batu in his place.

While Erikaya still resisted concentric rings of Mongol troops, Chingis moved towards the upper Wei valley, where the boundaries of the Tangut, the Chin and the southern Sung met, with the intention of invading Honan. Meanwhile he received a message from the king of the Tangut, suing for peace. He drew up a treaty requiring him to surrender Erikaya and do homage within a month.

At this point Chingis was taken ill again with high fever and saw that his end was near. He announced that Ögödei was to succeed him: Börtei was to be regent until the *kuriltai* met to elect Ögödei, and Tolui between the *kuriltai* and the enthronement. The king of Tangut was to be executed when he arrived, his people were to be enslaved and Erikaya was to be razed to the ground. Tolui was to negotiate free passage through the Sung territory to attack Honan in the rear.

Plate 10 Chingis died on August 24th. His body was taken to Mongolia and buried in a secret grove on Burkhan Khaldun.

MUKALI IN CHINA

During Chingis's campaign in the west, military operations in China were carried on under Mukali, who was subject to the remote control of his master in political matters. Mukali's force, perhaps seventy thousand strong, contained nearly half that number of Khitans and Chinese, who were needed chiefly as engineers for the continual sieges. Divisions of the force marched through fertile and densely populated regions separated by mountains, operating by siege and devastation and very rarely by pitched battles. The campaign began in autumn 1217 with offensives in eastern Hopei with Shantung, in western and southern Hopei and in Shansi. The Chin had made a counter-attack in Hopei, but in 1218 they were driven back there, while Shansi was subdued by a southward thrust down the valleys of the Fen and the middle Huang Ho. Mukali was persuaded by a captured Chinese general to make operations easier and more profitable by forbidding pillage and indiscriminate slaughter and by releasing prisoners.

In 1221 Mukali concerted with the Sung a great drive to destroy the western flank of the Chin. The ambassadors of the Chin had returned from meeting Chingis on the Amu Darya with a demand for all territory north of the Huang Ho. Mukali, accompanied at first by a Tangut force which later left him, marched through the eastern Ordos and Shensi, west of the Huang Ho. With great effort he defeated two large Chin armies, but could not take the most important towns. During a new offensive in Shansi he died in April 1223.

He was succeeded by his son Boru, who continued to fight over the same ground while the Sung kept up their attacks from the south. Boru in turn died in 1228, leaving the Chin state still surviving under the new Emperor Ai-tsung. So much more obstinately did the Chin resist than any other state that Chingis attacked.

CHINGIS KHAN IN HISTORY

As a leader and conqueror Chingis ranks with Alexander and Napoleon, though his methods were those of his fellow-nomads *Fig. 17,* Plate 38a Attila and Timur. His armies were not overwhelmingly numerous, though their mobility often made them appear so. His cruelty had been learnt in a hard school, among peoples whose traditions included tribal massacre after a conclusive victory. His religious vision of destined rule over the world was an extreme example of the belief in historic mission which has been a commonplace even among Christian rulers down to recent times, not to speak of rulers still more recent. His atrocities and those of his successors have been equalled in our own time, in Europe as well as in Asia, by men who had not been reared as nomads beyond the limits of the civilized world. His respect for such men as Ye-liu Chu-tsai and the Taoist sage Chang Chun, whom he summoned from north China to visit him on the borders of India and kept long in conversation, shows that with another upbringing he might not have been remembered mainly for the blood that he shed.

Fig. 17   Silver coin of Chingis Khan, struck in Afghanistan c. 1220. Obv. 'Commander of the Faithful', usual for Caliphs but an empty form for Chingis, who was no Moslem. Rev. 'The Just, the Supreme Chingis Khan'. 2 : 1. (British Museum. See also Plate 38a)

CHAPTER III

The Heirs of Chingis Khan

ÖGÖDEI 1229–41

AFTER THE TREMENDOUS career of Chingis Khan, Mongol history loses its initial momentum, for none of his successors had his military and organizing genius. But once the Mongol nation and army had been cast in their historic mould, the United Empire of the Great Khans was still of unique importance for much of Asia.

Chingis nominated Ögödei because of his shrewd understand- Plates 11, 13 ing of men and because of his amiable character, which would win willing obedience from others who could carry on the system. Ye-liu Chu-tsai, who saw that no other Khan would permit him to civilize Mongol rule, persuaded Tolui and Jaghatai to accept him at the *kuriltai* called in 1229 at Karakorum.

Chingis had divided the Empire into subordinate *ulusut* for his sons to rule under Ögödei. Jöchi had received the lands stretching westward from the Irtysh and the Aral Sea towards Russia; his son Batu had still to conquer these definitively. Jaghatai had received the territory reaching eastward from the Amu Darya towards China and Mongolia, except for the region east of the Ili, which was assigned personally to Ögödei. Tolui had received the Mongolian homeland, while under him his uncles Khasar and Temüge held north-east Mongolia and Manchuria.

The next business was to decide on further conquests and the completion of tasks unfinished. In Iran, Jelal-ad-Din had re-appeared and recovered much of his father's realm. In Russia the Bulgars of the Volga needed to be reconquered and the north Russian princes, though defeated, were still unsubdued. The most urgent line of action was agreed to be a new offensive against the Chin.

When a Chin embassy appeared hoping for peace, Ögödei refused outright. The Chin then prepared to defend the lower Huang Ho valley with a line of forts running south-westward from the Tung Kuan and manned by a hundred thousand troops. Their main army of two hundred thousand was drawn up in depth along the Huang Ho from Lo-yang to Pei-chou.

In 1230 the Mongols attacked in eastern Kansu, but were beaten off. Ögödei returned to his father's plan of arranging a passage through Sung territory, which was eventually granted. Tolui seized two passes leading eastward to the Wei valley while Ögödei attacked southward in Shansi. When Tolui had overrun Ssechuan, the Mongols, advancing southward and eastward on Ta-liang, destroyed a Chin army of a hundred and fifty thousand at Kun-chou in 1232. The Chin were forced to withdraw all troops to defend Ta-liang itself.

Sübüdei began the siege in the summer of 1232. At first the Mongols were baffled by iron land-mines full of gunpowder dropped among their sappers, by flying fire-spears propelled by gunpowder, by catapults hurling huge stones and by their own arrows blown back at them through tubes. Meanwhile Ögödei fell ill and Tolui died. Sübüdei, now in supreme command, negotiated for help with the Sung, who sent twenty thousand men under Meng Hung to join the siege.

In Ta-liang hunger and sickness began to undermine resis-tance. In 1233 Ai-tsung fled eastward to Kuei-te, while his family was handed over to the Mongols in token of surrender by Tsui Lui, who had usurped command. Sübüdei killed all the males, along with dignitaries also handed over, and asked permission to slaughter the rest of the inhabitants. Ye-liu Chu-tsai persuaded Ögödei to kill only the members of the royal clan, Wan-yen. Ai-tsung fled further, but was caught and killed himself. The Mongols and the Sung divided his bones.

In 1234 the Mongols withdrew northward with their captives, hunting down the conquered until Ye-lui Chu-tsai put a stop to it. The Sung Emperor, Li-tsung, was persuaded by irresponsible advisers to send armies northward to reassert the Sung claim to the former territory of the Chin. In 1235 Ögödei was preparing to punish the Sung, but he died before taking serious action here.

At the same *kuriltai* of 1235 Ögödei had decided on war in Korea, in Iran, against the Caliph of Baghdad, and in Russia. Korea had been nominally subjected in 1218 and thereafter intermittently raided until the king was again attacked in 1231 for refusing demands. The land was divided among Mongol officials and still plundered. But before more action was taken Ögödei's attention was drawn elsewhere.

In Iran, Jelal-ad-Din had been active even before the death of Chingis, leaving governors in his Indian possessions. By 1225 he had won a large following in Kerman and Shiraz, in Khurasan and Mazenderan, and had begun to move against Caliph Nasir of Baghdad. But Nasir was defended by Turkish and Arab princes. Jelal turned away to occupy Azerbaijan and to invade Georgia. He won two battles and took Tiflis, where he cherished the Moslems and massacred many Christians.

Warned against Jelal, the Mongols sent a force to put him down, but this was defeated at Damghan. In 1228 a Mongol force of five *tümens* destroyed half his army near Ispahan, but itself suffered so much that it left Iran. Jelal, who had escaped with difficulty, reappeared and again raised an army to dominate Armenia and Iraq. About the same time Nasir died and his successor Mostassem invested Jelal with the rule of Iran, but not of Iraq. Jelal now attempted to ally himself with the Seljuk Sultan Kaikobad of Rum for the joint defence of Islam, but he and the Sultan fell out over a matter in dispute and the Seljuk joined his Moslem enemies in a war against him. Jelal was defeated and fled to Azerbaijan, but still received a promise of support if he would lead Islam against the Mongols. At this point a force of three *tümens* under Chormagan arrived to re-conquer and occupy Iran and neighbouring countries. Jelal's support fell away until he was finally murdered as a fugitive in 1231 by a Kurdish tribesman. Though he was cruel and in-calculable and his Khwarazmian soldiers became a by-word throughout the Near East, he was unsurpassed in resistance to the Mongols.

The Mongols, finding no organized resistance, ravaged north-western Iran, northern Iraq, Armenia and Azerbaijan, collecting enormous booty at the fall of Tabriz, and imposing annual tribute. In eastern Iran, which had not rebelled, Mongol administration proceeded with Mongols in charge of districts and Moslems as emirs of towns. In 1238 Chormagan and his son Baiju in hard fighting defeated the Arab princes of Iraq. In Armenia they took Kars and Ani, the old capital, sparing only the craftsmen and children to be carried off. But in 1240 the Armenian prince Arak secured an order from Ögödei that the princes should be restored to their lands. In 1238 Transcaucasian Albania and Georgia had been overrun, Tiflis taken, and Queen Rusudani driven to take refuge in the mountains of Imeretia.

But the most famous of all the campaigns fought under Ögödei was the renewed invasion of Russia, directed by Sübüdei in the interest of Batu. In addition to his own troops, Batu received one-fifth of the Mongol troops from every other *ulus*, but even so his Mongols, numbering perhaps fifty thousand, were reinforced by some seventy thousand Turks under Mongol officers. Among his commanders were Ögödei's sons Güyük and Kadan, and Tolui's son Möngke.

Fig. 18

In 1236 operations began against the Bulgars and other peoples on the fringes of Russia. In 1237 the main army drove the Bulgars into Russia, while Möngke attacked the Cumans on the lower Volga and the Don. During the winter of 1237–38 the Mongols took Ryazan, Kolomna, Moscow, Vladimir, Suzdal, Rostov, Yaroslavl, Pereyaslavl Zalessky, Tver and many other places. They destroyed the army of the Grand Duke Yuri on the Sit, Yuri perishing in the battle. Only the spring thaw, certain to

Fig. 18   Chinese drawing of Batu Khan (after Iakoubovski-Grekov)

make impassable mud, prevented them from reaching Novgorod and the Baltic coast. Sübüdei turned the army southward, through undevastated country where more provisions could be found, to the basin of the Don, where the troops took a long rest, feeding up their exhausted horses and receiving others captured from the Cumans.

During this rest, dissension came to a head among the other princes, who resented their subordination to Batu. Güyük in particular was so insulting that Ögödei summoned him back to Mongolia. He was still Batu's enemy when he became Great Khan.

In 1238 the Cuman Khan Kotyan, who had fled westward with two hundred thousand men, women and children, was allowed by King Bela of Hungary to enter the Hungarian plain on condition that these became subjects and Catholics. While the Mongols operated on the Kama and Oka and in the Ukraine and the Crimea, Batu warned the Hungarians of the conse-quences of befriending Kotyan.

In 1240 the Mongols advanced on Kiev under Möngke. In December, when Batu arrived, it was taken by assault, but Prince Dmitri, who had defended it, was saved alive by Batu for his valour. So ended the old Russian state founded by the Varangians.

The Mongols pressed on through Volhynia and Podolia towards Poland and Hungary. Kaidu and Baidar advanced against the Poles, Kadan into southern Hungary along the Carpathians, and Batu and Sübüdei with the central army towards Pesth and Gran the chief cities of Hungary.

Bela attempted to block the Carpathian passes, but the Mongols broke through and butchered his garrisons. By the middle of March the first *tümen* had reached Pesth, cutting the country into two halves which could not communicate. Kadan's group meanwhile entered the plain on the south by two routes.

In the north Kaidu's group defeated the Polish army at Chmielnik and then pressed on in four separate thrusts to converge on Breslau, while a fifth column overran Lithuania and East Prussia.

At Wahlstatt near Liegnitz Archduke Henry of Silesia, who led the knights, cavalry and infantry of Silesia, Poland and Moravia, was attacked by Kaidu's force before he could join the Bohemian army of Wenceslas. His army was overwhelmed with arrows and by a well-placed ambush, and more than thirty thousand were massacred. His head was carried round the walls of Liegnitz. Wenceslas turned back with his fifty thousand to join the armies of Thuringia and Saxony. When his other army returned from Lithuania and Prussia, Kaidu moved southward to join Batu.

While the Cumans, who had now fallen out with the Hungarians, escaped to Bulgaria, the Mongols ravaged the country about Pesth until Bela marched north-eastward to fight a decisive battle. Near the junction of the Sayo and the Theiss he found Batu's camp protected by woods. But before he could attack, the Mongols forced their way by night across the only bridge over the Sayo and surrounded the Hungarian camp at Mohi. They assailed the camp with shot, arrows and burning naphtha until the Hungarians yielded, and cut them down as they fled. Bela escaped, but the other commanders perished.

Plate 27

Plate 28
Plate 29

All Hungary fell to the Mongols, who now divided the land, struck coins and appointed officials as if for permanent occupation. They remained in Hungary until 1241, while the other rulers of Europe gave up the country for lost. Bela was pursued through Croatia and Dalmatia to the island of Tran in the Adriatic, when the pursuit was suddenly called off, and threatened offensives in Austria and Bohemia were halted.

A courier had brought Batu the news that Ögödei was dead. He had died on December 11th, 1241. By the accepted rule, Batu was bound to attend the election of a new Great Khan. Unwillingly he made his way down the Danube to Bulgaria and Russia, while some of his troops ravaged Albania, Dalmatia

75

and Serbia. This was to be the limit of westward advance for the Mongols. Ögödei's death at this moment saved western Europe from an invasion which would surely have reached the Atlantic.

Ögödei had undermined his health by excessive drinking, like other Mongol Khans, except Chingis, and by continued sexual indulgence. It was an advantage to civilization that he was much less rigorously devoted to Mongol tradition than Jaghatai, who made himself the guardian of the Yasa in all its detail, and also much more open to the advice of officials who were not Mongols.

His reign covers the beginnings of civil administration under the Mongols. In the civilized countries that were overrun, Mongol arrangements were superimposed on systems inherited from earlier times in such a manner as to maintain the Great Khan's power but to alter little on lower levels. On the steppes the earlier institutions of nomads akin to the Mongols were adapted to the gigantic new framework.

At Ögödei's death the nomad foundation of the Empire was complete over the whole of the northern steppes. It consisted of the Mongol nation, numbering perhaps a million, men, women and children, and in a secondary degree of Turks and other nomads, who were more numerous and supplied the lower ranks of the armies outside Mongolia. Each of Chingis's sons, except the paramount Ögödei, had received his great *ulus* to govern as a state forming part of the Great Khan's empire, and also drew income and troops from some parts of the *ulusut* of the others, so that these dominions were interlocked under central control. Like the Great Khan himself, each possessed personal domains, or *inje*, which supplied the needs of his court; so did lesser members of the Golden Kin, while the great *noyat* received fiefs called *kubi*. Usually an *inju* was an area of steppe, but, where it included settled land, the prince received only a proportion of the tax on it collected for the Great Khan. Princes and *noyat* could, however, command feudal services in their domains.

Fig. 19 Two sides of Mongol paitza with inscription in the Uighur alphabet, found near the Dnieper. Length 26.5 cm. (after Yule-Cordier)

Under the regional Khans were *noyat* of varying degrees, ruling directly over *tümens* of households established locally in the final phase of conquest. In nomad territories, civil and military authority was hardly separable, since nomads of military age were soldiers. In settled lands, the administrative structure rested on the *darughachis* (in Turkish, *baskaks*) who collected taxes and enforced orders. These had local troops of their own but could call on the Mongol commander at need.

An important part of the Great Khan's services was the imperial post or *yam*, which carried orders and reports, and could also be used for transport by travelling officials and foreign ambassadors, who held *päitze*, or tablets of authority, differing with their ranks. A fixed number of horses, brood mares and sheep for meat was kept at each station; the horses were ready for instant use as relays.

Fig. 19

The taxes consisted of annual tribute to the Mongols and of the regular taxes, the *tamga* for merchants and craftsmen, the *kopchur* paid in animals by nomads and cattle breeders, and the *kalan* or land-tax levied on cultivators.

Among expert advisers at the centre, Ögödei employed Ye-liu Chu-tsai, the Uighur Chinkai, and Mahmud Yalavach, a

Fig. 20   Silver coin of the Great Khans, struck in north-west Persia c. 1240. Obv. 'There is no god but Allah; Muhammad is the messenger of Allah'. Rev. 'Ka'an, the Just', below: a bow, symbol of Mongol power. 2 : 1. (British Museum. See also Plate 38b)

Moslem Turk from Khwarazm. Yeʹliu Chuʹtsai was authorized
to hold examinations for the public service in the Chinese manner
even for prisoners and slaves. Thus he freed more than four
thousand learned men, who became judges or officials. He *Fig. 20,* Plate 38b
deprived local governors of their arbitrary powers and made
embezzlement and squandering of public funds capital offences.
He set up a system of courts of justice under a supreme court. He
founded schools to instruct Mongol children in Chinese learning.
He imposed a fixed system of weights and measures and made a
moderate amount of paper money legal tender everywhere. Some
of these characteristically Chinese measures must have been
applied mainly in the east.

GÜYÜK 1246–48

Though Ögödei had designated his grandson Shiramun to
succeed him, his widow Töregene, after two years of regency, *Fig. 21,* Plate 38c
finally secured the election of her son Güyük against the will of
Batu and others. While regent she dismissed Yeʹliu Chuʹtsai,
who died shortly after, and also Chinkai and Mahmud, and
appointed another Moslem AbdʹarʹRahman, as chief adviser.

*Fig. 21   Silver coin struck at Tiflis, Georgia, 1244–5, during the regency of Queen
Töregene. Obv. 'There is no god but Allah ; Muhammad is the messenger of Allah'.
Rev. A galloping horseman drawing a bow at a bird ; below : a dog ; above : 'The Greatʹ
Mongol, Viceroy, CommanderʹinʹChief'. 2 : 1. (British Museum. See also Plate 38c)*

Fig. 22   Silver coin struck at Tiflis 1247 in the names of Güyük Khan and David Narin of Georgia. Obv. the king on horseback, right; above, left; date in Georgian majuscules 467 of Paschal Cycle (1247); right: monogram of King David. Rev. 'By the power of God, Dominion of Kuyuk Khan—Slave, David'. 2 : 1. (British Museum. See also Plate 38d)

During her regency Baiju, who had succeeded his sick father Chormagan, defeated the Seljuk Sultan Kilij Arslan at Köse Dagh, forcing him to submit. Hethum of Lesser Armenia also did homage, so that Mongol power now reached the Mediterranean on its Cilician coast. In the far west Batu, to whom the Russian princes swore allegiance, made his capital at Sarai on the Volga. He was formally subject to the Great Khans, but never did homage to Güyük.

Fig. 22, Plate 38d   In 1246 Güyük was finally enthroned at a *kuriltai* on the Orkhon. Carpini described how he was raised aloft with his wife on a great mat of felt among the assembled Mongol princes and grandees and the ambassadors and then placed on a golden throne. He was different from Ögödei: parsimonious, strict and unsmiling. He put Abd-ar-Rahman to death and reinstated Chinkai and Mahmud. To Europeans he is of interest for his diplomatic exchanges with the Papacy.[1]

Pope Innocent IV and the Christian princes of Europe were appalled by Batu's methods, but, because the Mongols had so devastatingly attacked Moslem powers, they hoped to join them in a new and more successful crusade and even to convert them. Some Christians still believed in the tales, probably spread by the Nestorians, of the great Christian monarch Prester John, who was preparing to attack the Saracens from the east. In any case an understanding with the Mongols seemed necessary to save Christendom, weakened as it was by the continuing feud between popes and emperors. The Council of Lyons met in June 1245 to consider Christian unity and defence against the Mongols. On his own account, Innocent sent off four missions to the Mongols, two of Franciscan, two of Dominican friars. The mission of John de Plano Carpini occupied the years 1245–47. His account of his journey and of the Mongols is supplemented by that of his companion Benedict. Though all the details are valuable, two features are specially important here: the reply of Güyük and the advice given by Carpini on his return. The Pope's letter was intended to be forwarded by Batu to the Great Khan, but Batu insisted that Carpini should himself go all the way.

The letter carried by Carpini reproached the Mongols in the name of Christ for their massacres and devastations and threat-ened them with the wrath of God if they would not stop. It asked what were the reasons for their conduct and what further they intended. Güyük must have known something of the contents of another letter, carried by the Dominican Louis of Portugal, which called upon the Mongols to acknowledge Jesus Christ and to worship his name in Christian fashion after instruction from the friars. The Pope's letter had to be translated from Latin into Persian and thence into Mongol: Güyük's went through the reverse process. The Pope and the Great Khan were far from understanding one another. Güyük took the Pope's letter as coming from a political ruler, under whom the princes were vassals, and as being an offer of submission. Some of his actual words deserve to be quoted:

'Furthermore, you have said that it would be well for us to receive baptism. You write to me in person about this matter and have addressed to me a request. This, your request, I cannot understand. Furthermore, you have written to me these words "You have attacked all the territories of the Magyars and the Christians, at which I am astonished. Tell me, what was their crime?" These your words we likewise cannot understand. Chingis Khan and Ögödei Khan both sent the Command of Heaven to make it known. But those whom you name would not believe the Command of Heaven. Those of whom you speak formed a great plan: they showed themselves presumptuous and slew our envoys. Therefore in these territories it is the Everlasting Heaven which has slain and annihilated these men. If not by the Command of Heaven, how can anyone conquer or slay out of his own strength?

'And when you say: "I am a Christian, I pray to God. I arraign and despise others," how do you know whom God absolves and to whom He allows His grace? How can you know it, that you speak such words?

'Thanks to the power of the Everlasting Heaven, all lands have been given to us from sunrise to sunset. How could anyone act otherwise than according to the Command of Heaven? Now you must say with upright heart: We will be your subjects and will place our powers at your disposal. You in person at the head of the monarchs, all of you without exception, must come to tender us service and pay us homage; then only will we recognize your submission. But if you do not obey the Command of Heaven and run counter to our orders, we shall know that you are our foe. That is what we have to tell you. If you fail to act in accordance with it, how can we foresee what will happen to you? Heaven alone knows.'

On his return, Carpini reported that the Mongols meant to conquer the world, and recommended that the Christians should face them in open war under one command. He warned against Mongol ruses in war and advised that all valuable things should be hidden in caves.

About the same time the Dominican missions of Ascelin, or Ezzelino, of Lombardy and André de Longjumeau set out, but went no further than the Near East.

In 1245 Ascelin was sent to the camp of Baiju on the Mughan Steppe. His journey took two years, probably because of difficulties in passing through Moslem Syria. In Tiflis he picked up Guichard of Cremona from the Dominican convent founded there in 1240. He spent two months with Baiju, who wished to send him to Mongolia, and was angry when he refused. Baiju was even more angry when he conveyed the Pope's rebukes and request for his conversion. He replied that Mongols would not make themselves dogs like the Christians and their Pope, and several times threatened him and his companion with death. He detained them while enquiries were made whether the Franks had crossed to Syria for another Crusade and while Eljigidei arrived from Mongolia to command against the Moslems. Finally Ascelin and his companions received a letter in the same terms as that handed to Carpini. They set off homeward accompanied by two envoys from the Mongols, Aibek, probably an Uighur, and Sargis, a Nestorian Christian. The Pope received the envoys with honour and sent back another letter of protest and regret.

André was sent in 1245 with orders to go to Tabriz and no further. Since he knew Arabic, he was well received by the Moslem princes of Baalbek and Homs, but to reach Mongol territory he had to make a circuitous journey by way of the Dead Sea and Upper Mesopotamia to Mosul, without betraying his destination. When he arrived at Tabriz he met the distinguished Nestorian monk Rabban Ata, but nothing is known of his dealings with the Mongols. He carried a letter requesting Rabban Ata to help the Pope in reuniting the Christians of Europe and Asia. Rabban Ata, who had been the respected friend of the Wang Khan and of Chingis, had used his position to save eastern Christians from Mongol cruelty and Moslem fanaticism. In his reply to the Pope, Rabban Ata exhorted him to end his feud with the Emperor Frederick II when Christians were being slaughtered and the Kingdom of Jerusalem had fallen.

At this time the Mongols were prepared to work with Christian powers against the Moslems. Eljigidei, who had orders to attack Baghdad, considered that Louis IX of France, if he invaded Egypt, as he intended, would divert the powerful Ayyubid Sultan and his Mameluk soldiers from helping the Caliph. He therefore sent an embassy led by two Nestorians from Mosul, David and Markus, to wait upon Louis at Nicosia in Cyprus in 1248. André, now with Louis, acted as interpreter. The letter from Eljigidei, probably drafted by a Persian secretary, showed none of the usual arrogance, but praised Louis as the 'sword of Christ', expressed the hope of seeing him in Asia, and asserted that Christians under Güyük everywhere enjoyed religious freedom without distinctions between churches. Louis in return sent a double embassy to Eljigidei and Güyük with letters and gifts. Both were to receive pieces of the true cross and Güyük also a chapel-tent of scarlet embroidered with scenes from the life of Christ.

While André was on his way as ambassador, Güyük died. After one meeting with Eljigidei, who no longer acted for the Great Khan, André and his companions passed on to the *ordu* of Ogul Gaimysh, the widow-regent, at Omyl east of Lake Ala-kul. She treated them as vassals bringing tribute, and demanded similar gifts every year, but made no promise of conversion or of equal alliance. The letter from Eljigidei had been deceitful, and Güyük had had the same designs as other Mongol Khans.

In pursuit of his western plans, Güyük had intended to subjugate Batu. When he set out in 1248, his way led through Batu's *ulus* where he could call on Batu's troops. Warned of Güyük's evil intentions by Surkukteni, widow of Tolui and mother of Möngke, Batu moved eastward with a large force to meet him. But before they could meet, Güyük, who was now a sick man, died suddenly on his way.

MÖNGKE 1251–59

Güyük's death brought a new crisis in the succession. Though Ogul Gaimysh became regent, Surkukteni and her sons joined Batu, who summoned a *kuriltai* in her camp. The *kuriltai* offered the throne to Batu. But he, unwilling to return to Mongolia, nominated his loyal friend Möngke, son of Tolui. The appointment was confirmed at a new *kuriltai* held in 1251 at the foot of Burkhan Khaldun. The house of Tolui was now supreme: the change brought some able rulers but also serious dangers.

Möngke was strict and parsimonious, and tried to restore the old simplicity of life among the Mongols. He was fair and considerate in taxation, waiving the collection of arrears and introducing a graduated incometax. Local revenues were used to maintain the local armies and postal services. Vassal princes were ordered to send troops only as tribute. But, as he had been educated by Surkukteni and had studied Yeliu Chutsai's methods, Möngke also understood civilization. He surrounded himself with sages, as foreign ambassadors found, and intended to build an observatory at Karakorum. He instructed a team of Persian, Uighur, Chinese, Tangut and Tibetan officials to prepare dictionaries of their own tongues. At court he kept permanent ambassadors from all parts of the world and representatives of all religions, whose services he and his family impartially attended.

Foreign conquests were to be continued in the spirit of Chingis. In China the Sung Empire was to be conquered; in the west,

Iran was to be pacified and the Caliph of Baghdad subjected. But Batu's *ulus* was not concerned, apart from supplying some troops. Möngke's youngest brother Arik Böge was to watch over Mongolia.

In China little progress had been made to carry out the decisions of 1235. But in 1246 Meng Hung had died and had been replaced by royal favourites.

There were still Mongol forces active in Ssechuan along the Upper Yangtse and in Honan and Hopei. In 1251 a new offensive was planned under Kubilai, the cleverest of Möngke's brothers, who was put in charge of all Chinese territories south of the Gobi. Kubilai had been educated by the Confucianist scholar Yao Chi, whom with other Chinese scholars and officials he consulted before leaving Karakorum. He even appointed another scholar, Chao Pi, to instruct young Mongols in Confucian doctrine and made him learn Mongol for teaching and for translation of Chinese books.

Kubilai was unwilling to attack the chief centre of Chinese culture, but held that the Sung state did not deserve to survive and that China should be reunited under the Mongols. In 1252 he took the field with Uriangkadai, son of Sübüdei, as his chief of staff, intending to kill as few people as possible. The war was to begin with an offensive in Ssechuan and Yunnan, for which Kubilai came south through Tangut territory to west Shansi and east Kansu.

Kubilai marched with the main force of seventy thousand by the basin of the Upper Yangtse westward over very mountainous country to the kingdom of Ta-li. The king, Tuan Hing-chi, was heavily defeated and went to Karakorum to do homage. Möngke spared him to rule Ta-li as a vassal with a political resident at his capital. Ta-li now became for the first time part of the Chinese Empire. Kubilai did not permit the usual massacre.

When Kubilai left for the north, Uriangkadai subdued the Man on the Upper Yangtse and the Thai and Shan tribes beyond. He thus conquered Yunnan, which had never before been part of China, and was honoured by Möngke in 1256. Returning southward, he overran the former Chinese province of Kiao-chi, then independent as the state of Annam under the Tran dynasty. By 1258 all south-west China, with these kingdoms added, was under Mongol rule, and the Sung were confined to the south-east.

At this time Möngke took the fateful decision to move the imperial capital from Karakorum, though this was not done in his lifetime. He ordered Kubilai to choose another site. Kubilai, with his particular interests and duties, consulted his Chinese advisers, and at first chose Lung-kang north-west of the Dolon Nor, where the Chin had had a castle. He called it Shang-tu, and later made his own summer residence there. Kubilai was now accused at court of conspiring in the interests of the Chinese. But when he went to Karakorum to clear himself, Möngke greeted him graciously and the proceedings were stopped. Yet those who initiated them represented a permanent faction among ruling Mongols, which later caused civil war.

In 1257 it was decided to destroy the Sung capital Lin-an, the modern Hang-chou. The ill treatment suffered in 1241 by an embassy of Ögödei was remembered and now made a *casus belli*. Möngke took command himself, leaving Arik Böge in Kara-korum. He marched with the main army into Ssechuan, while two armies under Kubilai marched, one to the Yangtse to threaten Lin-an, the other against King-shan to draw off part of the Sung army. Uriangkadai was to march north-eastward to join Kubilai. The Sung were then to be attacked from north-west and south at the same time.

The Mongols found unexpectedly strong resistance from the Sung, who had set up a defensive system in Kuangsi on the Lung-kiang. The Emperor Li-tsung was kept in ignorance about the western defences by his favourite, Tung Ta-tsuan, until this minister was exposed and executed in 1258. But the

Mongols had difficulty in reconquering Cheng-tu and other western regions. Möngke was held up at the siege of Ho-chou in the Kia-ling for the whole summer, until he retired sick to the mountains and died on August 11th, 1259.

The Mongols decided that they must return home for mourning and the customary *kuriltai*. Kubilai, after a victory, accepted an armistice with tribute only because he heard that Arik Böge in Karakorum was claiming the authority of Great Khan and had sent troops to Lung-kang. He marched northward to secure his own succession.

Fig. 23, Plate 38e

The other great enterprise of Möngke's reign was the definitive conquest of Western Asia. On this campaign Möngke despatched in 1255 his other brother Hülegü, with an army estimated at a hundred and twenty-nine thousand Mongols and Turks,

Plate 16

with one-fifth of every other Mongol force. A broad belt of pasture was cleared of nomads and their animals along the route from Zungaria to the Amu Darya, and engineers and experts in siege were drafted from China. In September Hülegü reached Samarkand and sent twelve thousand men under Ketböge to attack the Assassins in northern Iran. He summoned all the rulers of the territories assigned to him to do homage. The summons was answered by the two Seljuk Sultans of Rum and by the rulers of Herat, Fars, Iraq al Adjem, Khurasan, Azerbaijan, Arran, Shirvan and Georgia, all already overawed by Chormagan and Baiju, but there was no sign of submission from Ala-ad Din Muhammad, *Shaykh* of the Assassins or from Mostassem, the new Caliph of Baghdad.

Plate 17

Hülegü decided to move against the Assassins as soon as possible. This fanatical order of Isma'ili heretics, with its elaborate and subtle doctrine, had obedient devotees, the *fedayin*, who would murder any man, however exalted, who opposed their aims. No ruler had been able to destroy their power. From their main stronghold of Alamut in Kuhistan, they are said to have controlled three hundred and sixty mountain fortresses in northern

Fig. 23   Silver coin of Möngke, struck at Tiflis between 1252 and 1261. Obv. 'There is no god but Allah alone. He has no associate.' Rev. 'Mungke Ka'an, the Supreme, the Just.' 2 : 1. (British Museum. See also Plate 38e)

Iran and further west. After being delayed all the winter by snow, Hülegü sent a demand to the new *Shaykh*, Rokn-ad-Din Khur-shah, son and murderer of Muhammad, to surrender himself and dismantle his fortresses. When he did not appear, Hülegü sent three converging columns to besiege him in another great fortress, Maimundiz. He was forced by starvation to present himself, and ordered his other fortresses to surrender. Finally all the Assassins' fortresses in Iran were taken or starved out, includ-ing Alamut, which was besieged for three years. Hülegü sent Khurshah to Möngke, who had him executed on the way.

In 1257 Hülegü was ready to march on Baghdad. He sent a threatening letter, to which Mostassem merely replied with refusal and rebuke. Hülegü was furious, and announced that he would invade. The Caliph, who already felt that he was pro-tected by God against anything that Hülegü might do, was further persuaded to take this tone by one of his officers, the 'little *dewatdar*' Munjahid-ad-Din Aibek. He would not heed his vizier Muwied-ad-Din ben Akami, who advised surrender, but accused him of trying to win Mongol favour. A general, Suleiman Shah, mustered a large army, which out of avarice Mostassem left unpaid for five months, until it mutinied.

Hülegü attacked in 1257 from the Iranian mountains while Chormagan and Baiju, coming from Rum, closed in on the west. Some further troops were provided from the *ulus* of Jōchi.

The Caliph's army under Fath-ad-Din ibn Kerr, which had been on the east bank of the Tigris, crossed it to meet Baiju and Böge Timur. The Mongols destroyed a dam and flooded the plain behind their enemy. They then attacked the Caliph's troops and routed them, leaving a hundred and twenty thousand killed and more drowned in the mud. While the 'little *dewatdar*' with a few men escaped to Baghdad, Baiju's men reached the western suburbs and Hülegü and Ketböge completed the encirclement from the east by the beginning of 1258.

Within a trenched and walled ring the Mongols besieged Baghdad without respite until they breached the eastern wall by the Persian Tower. The Caliph's envoys were turned back and for six days the attack was pressed with stones from the mountains and sawn-off palm-trunks as missiles. Arrows were shot over the walls with messages offering to spare all who had not taken up arms. When the Persian Tower collapsed, the Mongols carried the rampart by storm, occupied the whole of the eastern city, and caught those who tried to escape by boat. Seeing the Mongols on top of the walls, the Caliph surrendered. His officers and soldiers were killed, and eight hundred thousand of the people, who came out to be counted, were massacred. The Caliph was forced to reveal the wealth accumulated in five centuries, which was piled round Hülegü's tent, and was finally trampled to death under the hoofs of horses.

The former vizier was appointed governor and the city rebuilt. Other town submitted and an enormous treasure was carried off to Azerbaijan, where Hülegü intended to keep his *ordu*. Three-fifths of it was promised to Möngke. Advancing into Syria, the

Plates 18, 19

Mongols took Aleppo and slaughtered the population except for craftsmen. Damascus and all Syria submitted. But as Hülegü prepared to attack the Sultan of Egypt, the news came that Möngke was dead. Hülegü took the road eastward, leaving Ketböge to continue operations with a relatively small force.

The other aspect of Möngke's reign that deserves mention is his relations with Catholic Europe. These are revealed mainly by William of Rubruck, who set out in 1253 as a missionary sent by Louis IX. Like Carpini, he was not instructed to go as far as Mongolia but was sent on by Batu. When he reached the *ordu* near Karakorum in 1254, exhausted with riding and suffering from the cold, Rubruck found that Möngke's interest in Christianity was academic, and that he was even required to debate with leaders of other religions. Leaving in 1254, he carried a letter from Möngke to Louis like that of Güyük to Innocent IV, which ended thus:

'Send us your ambassadors; and thus we shall judge whether you wish to be at peace with us or at war. When by the power of the Everlasting God, the entire world, from the rising to the setting of the sun, is but one in happiness and peace, then it will appear what we must do, if you have understood and grasped the commandment of the Everlasting God, and if you do not refuse to hear and believe, saying: "Our country is far off, our mountains are high, our sea is wide." And if, confident in this, you make war on us, the Everlasting God, who makes easy what was difficult and makes near what was far, knows that we know what our power is.'

Louis regretted that he had ever tried to treat with the Mongols, much more to convert the Great Khan. But Europe was once more saved when Kubilai, who had himself elected Great Khan in Kai-ping, found himself compelled to fight a civil war against Arik Böge, elected at Karakorum. There was never again to be a unified Mongol command acting in the spirit of Chingis.

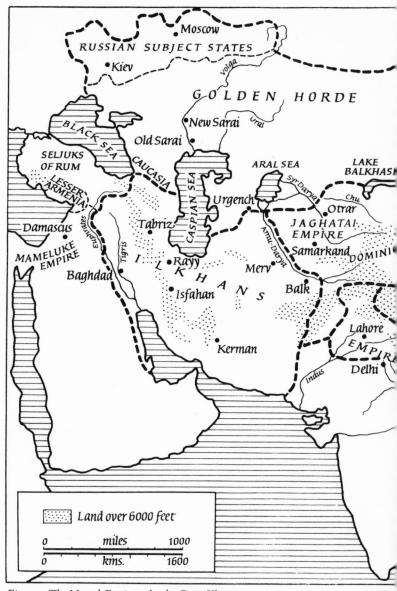

Fig. 24   The Mongol Empire under the Great Khans

Fig. 24

An account of the united Mongol Empire should not end without a description of its capital, Karakorum. The description of Rubruck can now be supplemented by the report of the Russian expedition that partly excavated the site during the years 1948 and 1949.[2] It found remains of buildings, tiles, architectural ornaments, pottery, coins and metal-work which make it clear that Karakorum was an important centre of trade and industry as well as of government. The town was a Mongol creation, like Sarai on the Volga, and deserves special notice in a book which has not room to describe far larger, more ancient and more famous cities that were for a time used as centres of Mongol power.

The site, on former Naiman territory, was apparently chosen by Chingis for a military centre and arsenal, but its development as a town with buildings was due to Ögödei, who also built the palace. Karakorum lay at the foot of the southern slope of the Hangai Mountains on the upper course of the Orkhon and near its right bank. This region had been for centuries a classic centre of nomad power and had even at times, as under the great Turkish Khans, contained cultivated land. The position of Karakorum was, after some centuries of oblivion, finally determined by excavation. This bore out the evidence of annals and inscriptions, confirmed the suggestions of the best scholars, and produced results that corresponded point by point with the description of the eye-witness Rubruck.

According to Rubruck, the town outside the palace was not at all impressive. There were two main quarters, one Saracen, which contained the markets and was thronged with merchants attracted by the court and the multitude of ambassadors, the other Chinese, which was full of craftsmen. Apart from these quarters were large palaces where the court's secretaries worked. There were twelve temples of idolaters of various nations, two Moham-medan mosques, and one Christian church on the edge of the town, which was enclosed by a brick wall with four gates. Near the eastern gate there was a bazaar for millet and other grains; near the western, for sheep and goats; near the southern for oxen and carts; by the northern, for horses.

Abutting on the walls, the Khan had a great court enclosed with a brick wall. Inside this enclosure was his palace, built like a church, with a central nave and two sides, each separated from this by two rows of columns, and with three doors on the south. The Khan sat on a couch raised on a dais at the northern end, so as to be visible to all. Two stairways led to this dais, by one of which his goblet was carried up and by the other carried down. The space between these stairways and his great silver tree (see below) was empty for the use of his cup-bearer and of the am-bassadors who brought him presents. He sat enthroned on high like a god, with his sons and brothers seated on a sort of terrace at his right and his wives and daughters at his left, excepting one wife who occupied a higher place near him.

Near the palace were several long buildings like barns, where the Khan's victuals and treasures were stored. In front of the entrance, where it would have been unseemly to carry in skins full of milk and drinks, stood a great tree of silver made by a captured craftsman Master Guillaume of Paris. At its foot were four silver lions each of which poured out white mare's milk through a tube in its mouth. Four pipes ran up inside the tree to the top; from this, drinks flowed down through the mouths of golden serpents whose tails coiled round the trunk. One pipe carried wine, one purified *kumiss*, one *boal,* a drink made of honey, and the fourth rice beer; a silver vat caught the flow from each. At the top of the tree was the silver figure of an angel holding a trumpet. A chamber at the bottom concealed a man whose duty was to blow through a tube reaching the angel whenever the chief cup-bearer needed more drinks: the angel then raised and sounded his trumpet. At this signal the cellarmen from a cellar outside the palace poured the appropriate drink into each channel of the tree. This ceremony was carried out twice a year at the Khan's drinking feasts when he passed that way in spring and late summer.

In Chinese records, Karakorum is called Ho-lin. They date the building of Ögödei's palace to 1235, a year before the town's walls were built to protect the wealth gathered by taxation and to act as customs barrier. Rashid reports that Ögödei, having established his court and his bureaucracy, decreed that his brothers and sons should erect palaces near his. Post-stations were built along the roads leading from it, and in it granaries to receive the freight of five hundred vehicles that arrived every day from the provinces loaded with edible stores and drinks. The vehicles were drawn each by eight bullocks and needed metal bushings for their axles because of the weight carried.

Two years' excavation naturally could not uncover the whole town, but a certain outline of its history was revealed. The main excavation was devoted to the palace and its attached buildings, but there were subsidiary excavations about the area of the town. The latter made it clear that the walls were not meant seriously as fortifications. The moat was hardly a metre and a half deep and only a metre wide, and the wall was not more than two metres high, though it had had a wattle fence along its top. The military power of the Mongols at this time made fortifications unnecessary for defence. The site of the town is roughly oblong, with a long axis running from north to south for 2,500 metres and a width of 1,500, diminishing southward.

An excavation at the eastern gates, through which ran the road to China, showed remains of a suburb reaching along both sides of the road beyond them. On the edge of this suburb stands the *Fig. 25* eastern one of a pair of huge granite tortoises, carved in Chinese style, on which a stone column once stood, inscribed probably with information for travellers. The eastern part of the site also contained remains of a long building six or seven metres wide, running inward from the gate-house and shaped like a corridor, which could be barred to control arriving travellers. From the

Fig. 25   Granite tortoise near the Palace at Karakorum. Very like the other, mentioned in the text, at the edge of the suburb, but rather better preserved. Both now have heaps of stones on them: they were once bases for stone stelae bearing official inscriptions. Approx. 6 m. long (after Kiselev)

high building of the main gate were remains of massive wooden pillars nearly half a metre thick which had rested on stone bases. Its walls seem to have been of vertical beams, 20 centimetres thick. In the entrance, where the guards would have been posted, was an admirably preserved brick warming/stove with a circular vent, from which flues under stone slabs had carried hot air and smoke round the building. Every possible kind of Mongol gaming/piece, made of bone, was found in abundance: these had served the guards during their ample leisure. To the south of this was found during some further excavations in 1950 a complete store of metal products, mainly agricultural implements.

The large and complex building called the House at the Crossroads had stood in the middle of the town; the parts of it most easily traced had faced on to back streets and it had been burned down twice and rebuilt in the same style. The roofs were tiled in bright colours and the lintels adorned with clay figures of stag/horned dragons; the walls were plastered inside and outside and painted with flowers, knuckle/bones and hieroglyphs. The heating apparatus was the same as in the eastern gate/house. Ten metallurgical furnaces were found in a small area. Among their

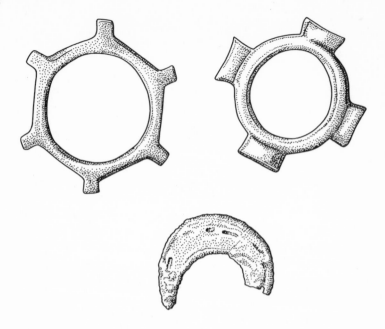

Fig. 26 *Two cast-iron axle-boxes for the wheels of great waggons that transported food and other supplies to Karakorum and carried the largest of the permanent mobile tents. External diameters approx. 9 cm. Below: an iron sickle. All from Karakorum (after Kiselev)*

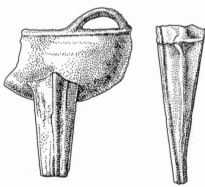

Fig. 27 *Pieces of three-footed iron cauldrons from Karakorum. Piece on the right is 20 cm. high, but the end of the foot has broken off (after Kiselev)*

products were wheel-boxes for the enormous wheels which had *Fig. 26*
carried siege engines and the great royal tents. A number of footed
cauldrons of white cast-iron had clearly been made for the army: *Fig. 27*
there were also arrowheads and sabres. The cast-iron was *Fig. 28*
examined by experts of the Steel Institute at Moscow, who reported
that no hand-operated bellows could have produced it. The blast
required for the necessary heat must have been supplied by bellows
connected to water-wheels driven by water from the Orkhon.[3]
There is still a canal from the river and remains of channels and
ponds can be discerned. Remains of smiths' forges showed
channels under their bases through which air must have passed
under pressure. Near the forges were found wooden dies carved
with the word *idzhi*, meaning 'ordered' or 'decreed'; a mark of
royal authority.

Great quantities of pottery were found, some plain grey, some
elaborately glazed in cinnamon, olive, dark blue and pale blue.
Some was still in the kilns. The ceramic industry was carried on
by master potters and workmen brought from China. Merchants'
weights and a great number of Chinese coins of various dates were
picked up. Ploughshares and mould-boards again indicate
agriculture, and great quantities of animal bones were evidence of
butchery.

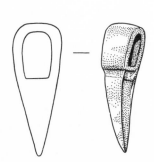

*Fig. 28   Iron implements from Karakorum.
Left: two views of pick head; 19.5 cm. long.
Right: mattock, 20 cm. long (after Kiselev)*

Fig. 29

But the main objective was the palace and its surroundings. The palace was built on artificially raised ground which appears now as a great flat mound, made of alternate layers of earth and sand trampled into a mass dense enough to make hard work for a pickaxe. Enclosing the palace was a four-sided court, built on an axis running from N.W. to S.E., with walls that are estimated to have been 4 or 5 metres high, made of clay, sand and pebbles, and perhaps faced with brick, though there are no traces of this. There were three walls, one inside the other. The outermost wall enclosed a space measuring 250 metres from north-west to south-east and 225 metres in width.

The great mound on which the palace stood measured 80 metres from north to south and 55 from east to west, and was perhaps once 3 metres high. Trenches dug in its surface defined the lines of its walls, making a rectangle 45 by 35 metres. To the west and east of the great mound were smaller rectangular mounds on parallel axes, one being now 2½ metres high, from 30 to 40 metres long and from 25 to 30 metres wide. These are likely to have carried the storehouses mentioned by Rubruck. On the eastern side of the palace was a low circular mound about 28 metres in diameter, which may have been the camping site for the Khan's great *yurt*, where he would have enjoyed the traditional domesticity of a Mongol during his hours of leisure. North of the main mound was a smaller mound, about 2½ metres high, 38 metres from west-south-west to east-north-east, and

Plate 12

25 metres across. This appears to have carried a domestic pavilion, joined to the main palace by a raised pathway which perhaps supported a connecting gallery. It had strong wooden pillars, like the main palace, and a wooden floor of beams, each 6 metres long, lying on cross-beams laid at intervals of 2 metres, and a roof of glazed tiles. Under the floor were found pieces of unglazed or dully coloured pottery, cast-iron cauldrons and animal bones.

The gate building to the south was more than 30 metres wide: it had a roof of two or more tiers, ornamented with yellow, blue and

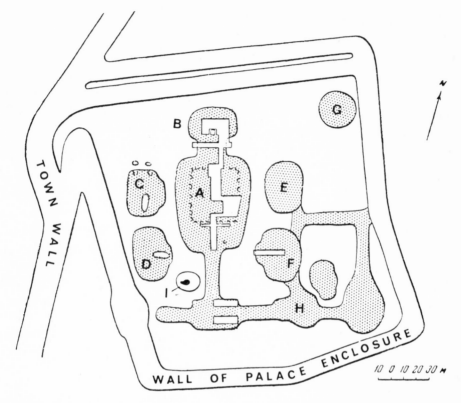

Fig. 29   Plan of the Palace at Karakorum, as revealed by excavation and indicated in text. Shaded areas represent raised ground. A, site of main palace; B, site of private apartments behind main palace (i.e. northern pavilion); C-F, storehouses or treasuries; G, possible site of the Khan's Great Yurt; H, gate and guardhouse and other buildings of uncertain use; I, stone tortoise (after Kiselev)

red tiles and resting on an undetermined number of strong wooden pillars. The entrance-hall, perhaps 15 metres wide and equipped with three gates, was apparently decorated with gilded figures of bears and lions, and to judge from a remaining foot, with statues or with human figures in high relief. The roof was decorated with figures of curled dragons with scales, wings and claws, all painted green and yellow. Beyond the gates the ground rose towards the palace itself.

The details of the palace have been conjecturally reconstructed from the analogy of Chinese and later Mongol buildings as well as from the account of Rubruck and from the comparatively scanty remains left when the site was subsequently cleared to provide materials for the neighbouring lamasery of Erdeni Tzu. It was a great building consisting of seven parallel colonnades under one roof. Its plan is defined by the remnants of rows of granite bases, usually about 1 metre square, on which rested great wooden pillars, estimated to have numbered seventy-two in all. Thirty pillars were enclosed in the line of the walls, indicated now by ditches, but forty-two supported the inner extent of the ceiling, which measured 55 by 45 metres. Thus there should have been six rows of seven pillars each, three on each side of a central nave; it is suggested that Rubruck did not observe the outermost rows nearest to the walls, not to speak of the pillars that were part of the walls and covered with their coating of plaster. The brickwork of the walls may not have been very high, perhaps only 3 metres; it may have reached little higher than the bottom of the windows. Above the brickwork wooden screens were probably set between the pillars, their surface broken by the decorated and mullioned windows.

The space above the windows was decorated with tracery close to the cornice, while under the roof there may have been a filling of timber or brick supported on wooden joists tenoned into mortices cut into the pillars. For so large a building a many-tiered roof is more likely than a single-tiered one; the inner and higher tiers would have been supported on taller pillars. The tiers would have been made in sagging curves of hemicylindrical tiles in the Chinese fashion, and sloped at their ends as well, leaving no vertical gables. To the brightly coloured green, red and dark blue glazed tiles were added sculptural adornments in the form of animals and dragons along the ridges of the roof.

The floor was paved with square brick tiles 34 centimetres square and 4 centimetres thick, covered with light green glaze except at the northern end, where they were left undecorated under the Khan's throne and the high seats of his family. This floor must have been intensely chilly in the Mongolian winter, and the palace must have needed heating by braziers like one found in the centre of the town, which had the form of a wide cast-iron dish. The columns were no doubt lacquered and engraved. Somewhere in the southern end must have been the great silver tree with its flowing drinks. The body of the hall must have been filled with courtiers, servants and ambassadors on whom the Khan and his family looked down from their raised platform.

A notable feature of this whole complex of buildings is that all of them were on raised platforms joined by raised pathways in a fashion which became common later in China under the Ming Dynasty. Ögödei's palace and its associated buildings may have been the first to be laid out in this manner. Thus during its brief career as an imperial capital Karakorum was a town which combined Mongol, Chinese and Central Asian features and quarters in a manner hardly known before.

CHAPTER IV

The Successor States

KUBILAI AND THE YÜAN DYNASTY

THE WAR BETWEEN KUBILAI and Arik Böge which followed their rival elections lasted until the latter was defeated in 1264. Arik Böge lived on in honourable captivity until 1266. In the west, Hülegü favoured Kubilai, and Berke, now Khan of Kipchak, supported Arik Böge. This division of sympathy re-appeared when Kaidu in Central Asia began a new war against Kubilai in 1268 and cut him off from the west.

The treaty that Kubilai made with the Sung on Möngke's death did not last long and was never properly ratified. Kubilai's envoy, sent to conclude details, was treacherously arrested and held by Kia Sse-tao, who did not wish his Emperor to know the real situation. In 1261 Kubilai declared that the Sung were to be superseded by his own dynasty, which should have the title Yüan and should rule from Chung-tu, now to be re-named Ta-tu, with a summer capital at Kai-ping, now to be called Shang-tu. All China was to be included in the new state. By the strategic plan settled with Chinese advisers, the Mongols were to close in southward and eastward by way of Siang-yang on the Han, An-hui between the Huai and the Yangtse, and Yang-chou, for a direct advance of Lin-an. In the meantime the Sung Emperor Li-tsung died and was succeeded by his younger brother's son, Tu-tsung, who was even more dominated by Kia Sse-tao.

In 1267, after Arik Böge was dead, Kubilai took final action. His generals A-shu Liu-cheng and Shi Tien-tse besieged Siang-yang. But the siege lasted for five years, because the city was victualled by the Sung from the east by junks sailing up the river.

Plate 15

These were protected by a bridge of boats and by the fortress of Fan-cheng on the northern bank. When Fan-cheng fell in 1272 to bombardment by giant catapults, Siang/yang was effectively surrounded. It was surrendered by its commander Lu Wan/huan, who was received with honour by Kubilai and appointed governor.

Further advance on Lin/an began in 1273 under Shi Tien/tse and the Mongol Bayan, who had been in Hülegü's service. Kubilai promised mercy to the innocent population if it did not resist. In 1274 Tu/Tsung died and was replaced by his four/year/old son with the Empress Sie as regent. Bayan and An/shu reduced all the towns as far as Kien/kang and continued in spite of Kaidu's advance into Mongolia. Four Mongol columns with Chinese and Alan contingents pressed on towards Lin/an, one by Tu Sung Kuan, one down the Yangtse, one by Chang/chou and the fourth through Hunan and Kiang/si. Kia Sse/tao was obliged to march in person against the Mongols. His army was broken at Ting/kia/chou near Yang/chou. Put on trial at Lin/an, he was removed from office, banished to Fu/kien and killed on the journey by the leader of his escort.

Other leaders continued the defence of Lin/an until in 1276, after various offers had been made, Bayan accepted surrender, but remained outside the walls and forbade his troops to enter and plunder. Public authorities were instructed to continue their routine, while the Empress and her son were summoned to Kubilai's court. They lived there in luxury until 1288, when they went to Tibet to study Buddhism and became monk and nun. The Imperial treasures of art and learning preserved at Lin/an were removed to Ta/tu, but the private property of scholars, and temples and great houses was not touched. The Sung had been overthrown with no small measure of humanity by the standards of the time.

In the far south two boys of the Imperial family, Shi of Yi and Ping of Kuang, had been rescued from Lin/an by Sung generals, who still continued resistance in South Kiangsi, Fukien, Kuangtung and part of Kuangsi. The fight was carried on until Shi, who had been proclaimed Emperor, died on the island of Kiang⁄chou off Wu⁄chuan in 1278. It was renewed when Ping was proclaimed, until the entire south⁄east coast fell to the Mongols and Ping was drowned in the sea with his last supporter. The Sung Dynasty thus ended altogether in 1279.

Kubilai had now stepped fully into the place of the Sons of Heaven, the historic Emperors of China. These had considered that their realm, *Chung Kuo*, the Middle Kingdom, was the civilized world, while beyond its frontiers were barbarians who must be made to respect the Imperial authority, and even, in periods of special vigour, incorporated. This attitude was taken over by Kubilai, who compared himself with the greatest of former emperors. He combined it with the Mongol doctrine of world⁄wide conquest by divine mission. He continued the programme of Chingis, but in a new way, claiming suzerainty of the world as of right, but at the same time hating violence and using it only when it seemed the only means. In the north this policy was identical with the unceasing war against Kaidu and his allies that any Great Khan would have had to wage. In the south and east it led to new wars beyond the limits of China.

In 1267, Kubilai sent his first embassy to claim submission from the Japanese.[1] This was foiled by storms at sea. Envoys sent on Kubilai's behalf by the king of Korea were turned back at Kamakura by officers of the *bakufu*, the military headquarters of the *shogun*, the real ruler of Japan, who would not allow them to go to Kyoto. When other embassies were turned back, Kubilai mustered in Korea a fleet of nine hundred ships with fifteen thousand seamen and ten thousand soldiers, too small a force for conquest but one intended to intimidate the *shogun*. It set out in 1274, occupied Tsushima and Iki and even landed on Kyushu, but in a bitter battle at Hakazaki ran out of arrows. Alarmed by a violent storm, it then returned home.

After other envoys had been executed at Kamakura in 1277, Kubilai declared Japan a province, and in 1281 sent a larger expedition of a hundred thousand soldiers on three thousand five hundred ships. Two separate fleets from Korea and from the Yangtse were to meet by a small island off Kyushu. After quarrels Plates 22–24 between the commanders and some bloody but indecisive en' counters with the Japanese, most of the ships were destroyed by a typhoon. The generals escaped and were pardoned, but their troops, left without equipment, were cut down until only thirty thousand were left to be captured and then killed or enslaved.

Another expedition was planned for 1286, but disaster else' where prevented it from sailing. The Japanese tradition has always made the most of these failures.

In the south, Kubilai aimed at extending Mongol rule from Ta'li over the kingdoms of south'eastern Asia. Except for Annam, which was Chinese in culture, these had Indian forms of culture, religion and art. Their rulers, though not Indian, used Sanskrit names and were Hindus or Buddhists. Annam and Champa were in the territory of modern Vietnam, and Mien in territory now belonging to Burma and Thailand.

In their campaigns of 1252–58 the Mongols had reached the frontier of Kao'chi or Annam and had imposed a political resident on the king, Tran Thai'tong. Tran Thai'tong, having bought peace in the north with tribute, attacked Champa and made it a vassal state. He found Kubilai's other terms for peace irksome, and tried continually to alter them until he died in 1276. He was succeeded by his son, Tran Thanh'tong, who made difficulties about doing homage in person to Kubilai.

Kubilai received formal submission from Indravarman V of Champa. But in 1280 when the king declared himself too old to come for homage, he ordered his general Sügetü to make Champa a simple province. Indravarman's son, later Jaya Sinhavarman III, seized some Mongol envoys as they passed the coast of Champa to claim submission from Sien further south and from Malabar in India. In 1283 the army of Champa fought bitter battles against the Mongols in wet jungle until the invaders captured the fortress of Mu Cheng. But even so the Mongols were driven to retreat by fever and starvation. Another expedition under Kubilai's son, Togan, and Sügetü invaded through Annam, but had to turn back for lack of food, and in its retreat was attacked by the Annamites, losing Sügetü and half its number.

In 1287, in spite of tribute from Annam, Champa and Cam-bodia, Kubilai again attacked Annam with an army of a hundred thousand, raised at great cost to the Chinese. Hanoi fell, but the king escaped, and a supply fleet was destroyed by the Annamite fleet. This army too had to retreat and suffered enormous losses under Annamite attack on its way to Ssechuan. A new army was being raised against Annam in 1294 when Kubilai died.

Westward from Ta-li, the Mongols had meanwhile attacked Mien in northern Burma in 1275. Its king, Narasihapati, refused to come for homage and arrested a Mongol envoy. Sin Sie-ji, governor of Ta-li, advanced into Burma with a small force and defeated a Burmese army of forty thousand, which had infantry, cavalry and elephants. Finally a large force was sent into Burma commanded by the young prince Singtaur, who set out in 1283 and took Kaung-sin. Since the king would not submit, the Mongols advanced to Tagaung on the Irawaddy and garrisoned the area when they retreated. In 1287 Narasihapati was poisoned by his son Sihasura. After another Mongol army had advanced into Burma, Sihasura sent tribute in 1293 from a country which was still not conquered.

Further afield, Kubilai sent an envoy to demand tribute from Java. He returned branded in the face. In 1293 an army of twenty thousand was sent from southern China in a thousand ships. One Javanese prince, Tuan Vijaya, submitted, but his rival in the west, Hajji Katang, had to be defeated. Then Vijaya ambushed the Mongols as they retired. They escaped with difficulty, and there was no success in Java.

But smaller states in the Malay Archipelago sent tribute. Tribute was also demanded from various rulers in southern India and Ceylon, who formally acknowledged Kubilai as suzerain, no doubt with some hope of advantage.

In the north, Kaidu attacked Karakorum in 1277, but was beaten off by Bayan, who had been hastily sent to take command. Kaidu was, however, eagerly supported in Manchuria by Nayan, son of Temüge. In 1287 Kubilai took the field in person against Nayan's army, a hundred thousand strong, in Liao-tung. Directing operations from a platform supported by four ele-phants, Kubilai defeated Nayan with great slaughter, and captured and killed him. In 1289 Kaidu, who had actually occupied Karakorum, was defeated again by Bayan, but he fought on after Kubilai's death until he was defeated near Karakorum in 1301, and killed in flight. The rest of Ögödei's descendants then made peace with the house of Tolui.

Internally, Kubilai's reign was a period of peace and order and to such observers as Marco Polo, even of magnificence. The Chinese regarded Kubilai as a Son of Heaven, unlike his suc-cessors. But though he admired the Confucianist tradition, Kubilai was not Chinese and was probably ignorant of the Chinese language. He had to found his power on Mongol commanders and soldiers, whatever use he made of other troops. In civil administration he continued to use Uighurs and Moslems and even Europeans such as Marco Polo during his stay.[2] By the end of his reign, the population of China was officially divided into four categories in descending order of authority and privilege: first Mongols; second *se-mu-jen* or classified peoples, other foreigners in public employment; then *han-jen*, northern Chinese; lastly *nan-jen*, southern Chinese.

In 1271, when the Yüan Dynasty was proclaimed, Kubilai promulgated a new order, planned by YaoShu, called '*Tiao kuo* order of the state'. At the same time the administration was recast by Liu Ping-chung and Hu Heng in a strictly centralized form.

The central Chancellery now had permanent outposts in the eleven great provinces, where they replaced the former governors. So had the separate Council for War, directly under the Great Khan, and the Censor's office, which controlled establishment and discipline in all branches of government. To the earlier provinces were added southern Mongolia, southern Manchuria, Korea and Yünnan, made from the kingdom of Ta-li. The army was divided into two categories: the *sui-wei*, which included the best Mongol and foreign troops of the Palace Guard and the provincial capitals, and the *chen-shu*, provincial and frontier troops under Mongol officers assigned to policing and other duties. For those who were not Mongols there was officially no conscription, but many were hired as mercenaries and many more must have been somehow compelled to serve in the wars.

Fig. 30

For official documents, coins and inscriptions, Kubilai introduced an alphabet invented by the Tibetan lama Phagspa.[3] The new script failed to displace Chinese and the Uighur scripts, and went rapidly out of use after Kubilai's time. Among languages, Mongol was used as much as possible by the higher officials, and Persian and Turkish were common among the *se-mu-jen*. Marco Polo needed only these three languages, and may never have learned Chinese. In religious affairs there were special ministries for Buddhism, Taoism, Islam and Christianity, as well as Confucianism. Jews and Manichees were tolerated. But the original shamanism of the Mongols, together with magical practices drawn from Tibet and Kashmir, remained essential at court.

Kubilai himself had a great respect for Buddhism, apart from his use of lamas to control Tibet. He, like later emperors, spent immense sums on building Buddhist temples and lamaseries. Tibetan lamas became a favoured class, much hated for their power, arrogance, and greed. At a higher level, Phagspa was nominated Teacher of the Realm *(kuo shi)* in 1260, and before he returned to Tibet in 1274 had made Buddhism a part of

Fig. 30   Cast bronze coin of the Yüan dynasty of China, late thirteenth or early fourteenth century. Inscriptions in Phagspa: 'Valid coin of the Chi Yuan period'. 2 : 1. (British Museum)

Mongol life which long outlasted the Yüan. At the lamas' suggestion Kubilai withdrew the privileges which Chang Chun had won for Taoism from Chingis.

Islam was in disfavour with Kubilai because of such rules as that of slaughtering animals by cutting the throat, contrary to Mongol custom, and even more for the Koranic injunction of perpetual war against infidels. To Christianity in its Nestorian form he was always favourable. As protector of the Christians in Asia, he sent to Baghdad two Turco-Chinese Nestorian monks, Markus and Rabban Sauma. Markus later wielded great influence in the Ilkhan realm as the patriarch Yaballaha III. Rabban Sauma went on a historic mission to Europe in 1287, visiting Rome, Genoa and Florence and meeting Philip the Fair of France and Edward I of England. In the reverse direction, the friars Odoric of Pordenone and John of Montecorvino tried to revive the missions of Carpini and Rubruck.

Communications by land were still carried across Asia by the *yam*, in spite of Kaidu. This service lasted until the fall of the Yüan.

By sea there was regular trade with southern Asia and Africa.

Within China ancient waterways were incorporated in the Grand Canal which linked Lin-an with Ta-tu and the Huang Ho, carrying large ships with supplies for the capital and the armies.

Like earlier emperors, Kubilai made use of paper money.[4] It represented a great range of values alike in coin and in un-minted metal and in quantities of silk, which were also used for exchange. The notes were compulsory tender; anyone who refused them was liable to execution. Their value depended on the emperor's power of enforcing their use; the weakening of this in later reigns brought increasing inflation. Foreign merchants arriving in China were paid in notes by the court and could then buy what they chose to take away. Corrupt operators made immense fortunes.

The wealth and luxury which so impressed Marco Polo were mainly a creation of the Sung, which Kubilai had taken care not to damage. Marco Polo saw the country with the eyes of a privileged foreigner. He describes vividly the great palace of Ta-tu with its hewn stone and marble, its walls and courtyards and halls, its treasure chambers, stores and arsenals; and also the summer

palace at Shang-tu, the Xanadu of Coleridge's *Kubla Khan*, Plate 36
surrounded by meadows and streams and a great game-reserve
and built of gilded and painted bamboo, so as to be transportable,
like a nomad camp.

When Kubilai died in 1294, full of years and honour but
without surviving sons, he left a great and dangerous legacy to
much inferior successors. Their tale must be quickly told.

A *kuriltai* attended by Kubilai's grandsons chose Kamala, but
as he preferred to keep watch on the northern frontier against
Kaidu, his brother Temür became Great Khan and Emperor.
Temür at once cancelled Kubilai's preparations for further war
against Annam, but he continued to exercise influence in Annam,
Champa, Mien and further afield, and to receive tribute. He was a
cautious and prudent ruler but unfortunately died of an illness
in 1307.

He was succeeded by Khaishan, nephew of Temür, who was Plate 37
known as a soldier but who as a ruler was a man of peace, a
benefactor of Buddhism and a promoter of Confucian studies.
After he died in 1311, Buyantu, brother of Khaishan, who had
the same policies and interests, ruled only until 1320. The next
emperors were Sudhipala (1320–23), Yesun Temür (1323–28),
Asikipa and Kushala (1328), and Togh Temür (1328–32);
all children or youths, dominated by Mongol ministers and
Buddhist lamas, and short-lived.

When Toghan Temür succeeded in 1338, Mongol grandees,
Chinese land-owners and Buddhist clergy between them had
prepared the ground for repeated peasant risings, while the quality
of the Mongol troops continually declined. Beyond the borders
of China the Yüan emperors no longer had any authority as
Great Khans. An attempt to strengthen Mongol power was made
by the minister Bayan, who enacted that all officials and judges
must be Mongols or *se-mu-jen* and that no Chinese was to learn
the Mongol or the Arabic script. He is even said to have proposed
in 1337 that all Chinese who bore certain common names should

be put to death. Bayan was deposed at the insistence of his nephew Tokhta, who restored the Confucian cults and public examinations, favoured Chinese culture and put in hand public works. But the risings and mutinies continued even after Tokhta was poisoned in 1356.

The most capable and constructive of the rebel leaders was Chu Yüan-chang. He decided to defeat all the other rebels and himself to deliver the final assault on the Yüan. He won over one province after another in southern China and set up his administration in Ying-tien, the later Nanking, where in 1367 he declared himself king of Wu. Two Mongol leaders in the north fought civil wars among themselves until the crown prince Ayusidhara took command. When Chu Yüan-chang had fought his way northward to the plain of Ta-tu, Toghan Temür decided to flee, disregarding appeals to defend his inheritance. He left suddenly with his family and suite for Shang-tu, and then in 1369 moved to Jehol, where he died in 1370. The dynasty had formally ended in 1368 when the general Su Ta entered the capital almost without bloodshed. Chu Yüan-chang announced that his new dynasty would be called Ming and himself took the name Hung Wu.

Thus ended the Mongol dominion in China, no less ingloriously than those of the Chin and the Sung. The victorious rising was directed only against Mongol grandees and those Chinese who had specially benefited from their rule. The *se-mu-jen* lost their offices, but not their lives. Mongols of lower degree continued to live in China and to serve in its armies. Both these Mongols and the *se-mu-jen* were slowly turned into Chinese over the generations.

The Yüan period was naturally inferior to the Sung period in intellectual and artistic culture, but outside the circles of Chinese *literati* there was a vigorous growth of popular drama and romance which suited unlearned Chinese and Mongol taste alike. Chinese art benefited in some degree from contact with Persian, though the reverse influence in Iran was greater and more important. Chinese science gained something from the Moslems, particularly in astronomy. Otherwise Chinese culture was little affected, since it had maintained itself by ignoring outer circumstances. The full development of non-classical literature was apparently checked by the Ming.

From the death of Möngke onward the Mongols in Iran pursued their own course, though suffering much interference from those of Central Asia and the Russian steppe. After leaving the Syrian front, Hülegü heard at Tabriz that Kubilai had been elected Great Khan. He approved warmly, but did not think it wise or necessary to advance further east in his support, especially as Berke Khan of Kipchak was his enemy beyond the Caucasus. In the meantime a decisive battle stopped the Mongol advance against Egypt.

Ketböge, commanding in Hülegü's absence, sent an embassy demanding submission from the Sultan of Egypt, the Mameluk Kutuz, who had usurped power on the death of an infant prince of the Ayubid line in 1250. Kutuz, like most of the Mameluk bodyguard, from which he came, was a Turkman from Kipchak. He and his Mameluks understood the Mongol technique of fighting, and were reinforced by the remnant of Jelal-ad-Din's Khwarazmians. After a council, Kutuz rejected the Mongol demand, gibbeted Ketböge's envoys and prepared for immediate war to forestall any stronger attack.

Ketböge advanced into Palestine with a force said to have numbered ten thousand, consisting mainly of Turks but under Mongol officers. On the 3rd September, 1260, the Mongols, whose advance guard had been checked at Gaza, met the army of Kutuz at 'Ain Jalut in Palestine. Kutuz sent a small part of his army under his general, Baibars, to draw the Mongols into an attack, which some Egyptian troops were left to face. He posted his Mameluks in ambush. Baibars's force fled before the Mongols, who advanced until the place of ambush was reached. The main army of the Mameluks then attacked the Mongols from all sides. The battle was equal until midday, when most of the Mongols broke and fled. Ketböge himself fought on for honour's sake until he was captured and led before Kutuz, who reviled him. He replied that one year's births among the people and horses of the Mongols would make up the losses of that day, and that the revenge of the Great Khan would be terrible. He asked to be beheaded before hearing any more reproaches. This was at once done.

The Mongol remnant was pursued through Syria to the Euphrates, which became the permanent frontier. On his way home Kutuz was murdered by Baibars. Under Bairbars and his successors the Mameluk power survived all Mongol attacks; it fell only to the Ottoman Turks in 1517.

Plate 38h

Hülegü's generals consolidated Mongol power in northern Mesopotamia and the country beyond as far as the Caucasus. The Ilkhans or 'obedient Khans', so-called because of their nominal relations to the Great Khan, became the rulers of an Iranian state with well-marked frontiers against other powers on the Euphrates, the Caucasus and the Amu Darya. Their immediate neighbours were enemies, now open, now concealed, and their most powerful friend was Kubilai, so long as he reigned. This pattern took shape during the rest of Hülegü's reign. Hülegü and his successors were repeatedly faced with alliance or cooperation against them between the Khans of Kipchak and the Mameluks in the west and the rulers of the *ulus* of Jaghatai in the east. Since Möngke had assigned Caucasia to the *ulus* of Jöchi, Berke, successor of Batu, claimed it as his territory. Berke had also other reasons for hostility; he had been converted to Islam and disliked the attack on Baghdad, and his contingent serving in that war had been so ungratefully treated that it had joined the Mameluks. In 1261,

Fig. 31   Bronze coin of Hülegü, struck at Irbil (Mesopotamia) 1262–3. Obv. in centre, a hare; above left, a crescent. Around, inscription: 'There is no god but Allah, Muhammad is the messenger of Allah'. Rev. 'Ka'an, the Supreme Hulagu Khan'. 2 : 1. (British Museum. See also Plate 38f)

since Hülegü would not yield, fighting broke out near Derbend and on the Kura and the Terek. Al Malik as-Salih of Mosul and King David V of Georgia also rebelled, but were crushed. In January 1263 Berke's troops won a great victory on the Terek, but could not drive Hülegü's troops out of Caucasia. The war on this front continued until Hülegü died and after, but the boundary between Ilkhans and the Kipchak Khans became fixed on the Caucasus.

In Asia Minor the Seljuks of Rum remained tributary. Michael VIII of Constantinople, whose father Manuel I had become in some degree a vassal of Möngke, concluded a secret treaty with Hülegü in 1261.

Since the main danger was now in the west, and Azerbaijan had the best pastures in Iran for an army of cavalry, Hülegü made Tabriz his centre of administration, where the vizier and other Fig. 31, Plate 38f officers worked with their staffs of clerks. He himself kept his *ordu* in the neighbourhood, during summer on the Alatagh, where he built a palace, during winter on the Mughan steppe. In 1265 he died suddenly after a banquet at the age of forty-eight and was buried in an immense tomb on the island of Sahi in Lake Urmia. He was succeeded by his son Abaka.

Under the system set up by Hülegü and his immediate successors, Mongol rule was direct only in Khurasan and elsewhere in northern Iran, except in Gilan, and in parts of Iraq. Fars, Kerman and Shabankara, with Hormuz and Qais on the Persian Gulf in the south, Luristan in the west, and Herat in the east, all continued within the Mongol framework under their native ruling families, who suffered little interference and in some cases outlasted the Ilkhans. Outside Iran, Georgia, Greater and Lesser Armenia and the Seljuk territories in eastern Asia Minor were dependent, but not under direct rule. Government was conducted in theory by the Khan and his *kuriltai* of Mongol grandees, but civil affairs even at the centre came to be handled by native viziers as in other Moslem countries. The heir to the throne was often set to govern Khurasan, if necessary, with an *atabeg* to guide him if he was very young, and with emirs to command the troops set to guard the Amu Darya. Provincial governors were mostly concerned with civil affairs, including police. Outside Iran, the Mongol governors were military commanders who left civil affairs to native authorities.

The central chancellery was modelled on that of the Great Khans, but naturally had many more Moslem officials. Supreme control of the state's income and expenditure was exercised by the Sahib-i-Divan or Grand Vizier, in later times often by two viziers. The vizier was also charged with postal services, public buildings, coinage and the registry of land. Coinage consisted of the gold *dinar* and the silver *dirham* inherited ultimately from the Arab caliphate and varying much in weight and purity. Taxation was on the same system as under the Great Khans, including cattle-tax, land-tax, poll-tax and sales-tax. The collectors, often venal and greedy, were supported on their rounds by military detachments. In indirectly ruled territories collection was assisted by *baskaks* who remitted a portion to the central government to maintain the army and the post.

In religious matters Hülegü was less impartial than most Mongol Khans. He did not persecute or insult Moslems as such, but could not like Islam, against which he had so long campaigned, and would not accept it as the religion of the state. Buddhism, which he had himself adopted, was a novelty introduced by Mongol power and a link with Eastern Asia. It had at first much influence and many temples. Christianity, also well known to the Mongols in its Nestorian form, was protected by Hülegü against the Moslems. Dokuz Khatun, Hülegü's favourite wife, was a Nestorian, and founded churches. The early Ilkhans gained a reputation in Europe as protectors of Christianity, which their successors still found useful.

The later history of the Ilkhans cannot be followed in detail here, but a brief outline can be traced under the heads of war and foreign relations, of religious policy and of internal politics. It shows a decline arrested by the reign of Ghazan, the ablest ruler after Hülegü, and then again decline and final dissolution. In foreign relations a certain cycle of events is repeated from reign to reign as one ruler after another attempts to extend Ilkhan power or to consolidate a frontier against obstinate enemies, who often act in concert.

When Abaka succeeded, the Kipchak army was still attacking in Caucasia under Nogai, but was finally beaten off. In the east, Borak of the House of Jaghatai, defeated by Kaidu, tried to compensate himself by invading Khurasan; meeting with no success, he returned to Bukhara, where he died by Kaidu's plotting. Nor could Abaka hold Bukhara when he occupied it. The frontier remained on the Amu Darya. In the west, Baibars invaded Lesser Armenia in Cilicia and tried to deliver the

Plate 30
Plate 38i

Moslems of Rum from the Mongols, but was defeated by the main Mongol army and returned in 1277 to Egypt, where he died. But Abaka's attempts to conquer Syria in 1278 and 1279 were not successful, so that the frontier remained on the Euphrates.

Abaka's brother Tekuder, who succeeded in 1281 and became a Moslem under the name of Ahmed, was none the less rebuffed in 1282 when he proposed friendship to the Mameluk sultan Kalawun. Abaka's son Arghun, an enemy of Islam and of Egypt, tried in 1289 to bring in the Christians of Europe by a letter to Philip the Fair of France, promising to hand over Jerusalem if he would help against the Mameluks.

Plate 31

Ghazan, the next effective ruler, who succeeded in 1295, held off another invasion from Transoxiana, In the west, his general Kutlugh Shah pressed back the Mameluks in Lesser Armenia, put down the rebellious governor Sulamish in Asia Minor, and brought to heel David VI of Georgia by installing beside him his brother David V, who was more loyal to the Ilkhans. In 1299 the Mameluk Al Malik al Nasir invaded northern Iraq. In a counter-attack Ghazan's troops reached Damascus, whose governor changed sides, but on the advance of an Egyptian army the same governor rejoined the Mameluks. Ghazan had to abandon all his gains beyond the Euphrates. Near the end of his reign he made another effort, when the Mameluks had deposed and blinded King Hethum of Lesser Armenia. Kutlughshah and Choban were sent into Syria, where they besieged Homs, but at Shakkab they suffered an annihilating defeat. In the north-west Tokhta of Kipchak renewed diplomatic pressure for the cession of Caucasia.

Fig. 32, Plate 38g

Ghazan's brother Öljeitü, who succeeded in 1304, was so elated by hearing that peace was restored in Transoxiana, that he sent embassies to Philip of France and Edward I of England to announce that the Mongol princes were in harmony and desired friendly relations with those of Europe.[5] But nothing came of this attempt to win Christian allies against the Mameluks. Turning

Fig. 32   Gold coin of Ghazan Mahmud, struck at Shiraz 1300–1. Obv. 'There is no god but Allah, Muhammad is the messenger of Allah'. Rev. inscription in Uigur : 'Struck by Ghazan by the Power of Heaven'. Between lines, in Arabic : 'Ghazan Mahmud'. To left, vertically, three characters in Phagspa (Ka'an ? Ghazan ?) 2 : 1. (British Museum. See also Plate 38g)

then to military action, Öljeitü sent his army to Mosul, but in 1312 it was compelled to retreat by failure of provisions and by sickness. In 1314 the Khans Köpek and Yasavur from Transoxiana invaded Khurasan, but were finally driven back to Bukhara. In Caucasia, Tokhta's threatening movements of troops did not result in war.

Abu Sa'id, succeeding in 1316, again found Köpek and Yasavur invading Khurasan. But Köpek later joined the Ilkhan commander in attacking Yasavur's army as it returned from the invasion. He captured and beheaded Yasavur. In the west, Choban dealt successfully with a rising of the Turkish princes of Asia Minor, and kept at bay Özbeg of Kipchak, who had begun to attack. But after the death of Choban, Özbeg had more success. By the end of the reign he occupied Azerbaijan as the Ilkhan realm fell to pieces.

Religious policy had a special importance under the Ilkhans. From being enemies and as far as possible persecutors of Islam, they became Moslem sovereigns who differed little from others. Abaka forbade conversion of the ruling Mongols and promoted Buddhism, to which many of these were attached. Among Christians, Markus, who arrived from China on pilgrimage to Jerusalem, was elected Nestorian Catholicos in 1281. During the reigns of seven rulers he wielded influence at court and protected Christians from Moslem persecution. Ahmed's conversion to Islam was a political move; it failed to conciliate the Mameluks and led to a Mongol rebellion which overthrew him. Out of hostility to Islam, Arghun favoured the Christians and restored the Nestorian Yaballaha to favour, but this was the last favourable moment for Christians under Ilkhan rule. Arghun was himself an increasingly fanatical and solitary Buddhist. The Jews suffered persecution when he died, because of the extortions of his Jewish vizier Sad-ad-Daula. Under Gaikhatu and Baidu the Mongol nobility, finding the dynasty too weak, gave up their resistance to Islam. Ghazan, determined to restore Ilkhan power, accepted Islam, followed by the nobility. Buddhist temples were destroyed and Buddhism vanished from Iran. Abu Sa'id was a Moslem from the first.

In their internal administration the Ilkhans had many misfortunes. Abaka was plagued by bitter enmity between Majd-al-Mulk, whom he promoted to be a vizier, and the existing viziers, the brothers Juvaini; this situation recurred in later reigns. Ahmed executed Majd-al-Mulk and reinstated Shams-ad-Din Juvaini, whom he had imprisoned. Under Arghun Shams-ad-Din Juvaini quarrelled with a new vizier, Böge, and was tried for corruption and unjustly condemned to death with all his family. Böge was executed in 1289 for favouring rebels, and after him, as Arghun lay on his sick-bed, the Jewish vizier Sad-ad-

Daula was put to death after a successful career of extortion.

Gaikhatu, brother of Arghun, became Khan because his Plate 32 spendthrift liberality as governor in Asia Minor had made him popular. As ruler he dissipated public funds in presents, at a time when the yield of the cattle-tax was ruined by disease among the herds. Worse followed when, on the advice of his vizier, he introduced paper-money on the Chinese model and forbade the use of coinage in exchange. Food ceased to be sold in the towns, whose people had to look for it in the country, until the ban on coin was removed. Gaikhatu's cousin Baidu was attacked by Ghazan, who on the advice of his follower Nauruz embraced Islam and was enthroned in November 1295.

Ghazan may be regarded as the second founder of the dynasty. Plate 33 He made it a ruling house independent of the Great Khan. A sign of this was the new Ilkhan era that he introduced, dated so as to run side by side with the Moslem. By ruthless executions he ended civil war. New coinage and weights and measures were introduced, and taxation was reformed. The pay and equipment of the army were set on a new basis, and communications re-organized. Among commanders, Nauruz fell out of favour through the slanders of his enemies and was finally put to death. During these disturbances Rashid-ad-Din was rapidly pro-moted to Grand Vizier; he was in office when Ghazan suddenly Plate 34 died in 1304.

Öljeitü, who tried to maintain the new regime, moved his Plate 38j capital to Sultaniye in 1307. Otherwise there was no change. The enmity of rival viziers continued, first between Sad-ad-Din Saweji and Rashid-ad-Din; then, after Saweji was executed, between Rashid and Taj-ad-Din Alishah. In these circum-stances Öljeitü was unable to prevent extortion and embezzlement in the highest places for the rest of his reign.

Under Abu Sa'id, Rashid, who had fallen out with Alishah, Plate 38k was executed in his turn. After this, Abu Sa'id was at first greatly dependent on Choban as commander and administrator, but became alienated when Choban refused him his married daughter's hand, and even more when Choban's son was caught with a royal concubine. The enemies of Choban used these opportunities to work against him while he was campaigning in Khurasan. He took fright, becoming first a rebel and then, as his commanders left him, a fugitive, until he was arrested at Herat and finally executed in 1327.

When the best ministers and officers suffered such fates, it is no wonder that administration under the Ilkhans was never satisfactory. After Abu Sa'id died in 1365 on the way to meet one of Özbeg's invasions, the male line of the Ilkhans came to an end. The Mongols attempted without success to hold the realm together under various rulers of other families. For a time the Jalairs ruled a small successorstate in Mesopotamia, while the rest of Iran fell to Persian or other princes who were not Mongols at all. After a successful invasion by Janibeg, Khan of Kipchak, in 1357, Berdibeg, his son, ruled for a short time in Tabriz, subsequently leaving a governor there. Conditions in Iran at this time were made even worse by the notorious plague, the Black Death.

In spite of their alien origin and their maladministration, the Ilkhans were among the promoters of Persian culture. Besides their native Mongol, they spoke and read Turkish and Persian and sometimes Arabic. Their buildings, including the observatory at Maragha, were noteworthy. In painting, the new PersianMongol style which arose under them had a vigour of its own, drawn from the stimulation which Uighur and Far Eastern art gave to the somewhat tired PersoArab tradition of the preceding period. Though many of the traditionally cultured ruling class of Iran lost their positions, literature at least gained something from the famous historical works of Juvaini and Rashid, which are valuable sources of reference for the entire history of Asia in this period.

THE HOUSE OF JAGHATAI IN CENTRAL ASIA

The *ulus* of Jaghatai had a more troubled history than any other division of the Mongol Empire. This was due, not merely to the pressures and rivalries of the greater dominions that enclosed it, but even more to the internal contrast between the predominantly settled Moslem population in its western part and the mostly nomad and Mongol population in the rest of it. It had in fact the same instability as the Khwarazmian and Karakhitai empires that it replaced. Its western part, though much of it was desert, contained the basins of the Amu Darya and Syr Darya, except where their lower ends had been assigned to the *ulus* of Jōchi, and also great cities, such as Bukhara and Samarkand, which were rebuilt after their devastation. The eastern part, except for cultivated lands by the Ili and other valleys of the Semirechye and the oases of the Tarim basin, consisted of steppes which were suited to the nomads. The *ordu* of Jaghatai and his first successors moved about the fertile Ili valley according to the time of year. Jaghatai was the most rigorous and conservative of Mongols. He disapproved bitterly of Islam, but was favourable to Christians and Buddhists.

Jaghatai removed Mahmud Yalavach, but Mahmud's son Masud Beg was appointed governor of the agricultural regions of Central Asia from the Uighur country to Khwarazm, and held office until 1289 through all the changes among the Khans. After the death of Jaghatai, his grandson Kara Hülegü ruled until the Great Khan Güyük replaced him by Yesu Möngke, a son of Jaghatai. But Möngke, when he became Great Khan, reinstated Kara Hülegü because Yesu Möngke had sided with Ögödei's sons against him. At the same time he removed all military chiefs who had been his enemies, and occupied all the territory between Karakorum and Bishbalik with his own troops. At this moment Kara Hülegü died, leaving the *ulus* without its own Khan and without control of its territory. On Möngke's death Arik Böge sent another grandson of Jaghatai, Alghuy, to hold the *ulus* for him. Alghuy resolutely took control, but not in Arik Böge's interest. Arik Böge went to war with him, but could not defeat him before he was abandoned by his generals and had to submit to Kubilai. Kubilai in turn recognized Alghuy as Khan of Jaghatai. But Berke of Kipchak would not recognize him, nor would Kaidu, the great enemy of Kubilai, in the north-east.

Alghuy died in 1265 and was succeeded by Mubarak Shah, son of Kara Hülegü, who was a Moslem. Since this happened without his consent, Kubilai sent Mubarak's cousin Borak to expel him. Borak was successful, but without Kubilai's authority

Plate 35

declared himself Khan. Kubilai now sent an army against him, which he defeated. Meanwhile Kaidu, representing Ögödei's line, seized the Semirechye as Borak's rival. The two came to an agreement in 1269 with Kaidu as senior partner. Kaidu there-after behaved in Central Asia as if he were Great Khan, fighting by turns against Kubilai, against the Ilkhans and even against Kipchak, thus more than any other breaking up the Mongol Empire.

Kaidu's son Chapar could not maintain the same power, and Tuva of the Jaghatai line became the most powerful ruler. On his death his son Köpek gathered effective power to himself, though another son, Esen Böge, was enthroned as Khan. Most of the lands seized by Kaidu were recovered by the Jaghatai princes, but Esen Böge's authority was weakened by the stress of frequent and not very successful warfare against the Yüan and the Ilkhans, to whom Yasavur, a prince of the family, went over. Köpek himself was the next Khan. He and his successors increasingly confined their interest to their Moslem dominions. His brother Tarmashirin became a Moslem, and was overthrown by a Mongol revolt in 1334. Among later rulers, Jenkshi and Yesun Timur were more favourable to their Mongol subjects and lived at Almalik on the Ili. They also welcomed Catholic missionaries. Yesun Temür was deposed by a rabid Moslem, Ali Sultan, who persecuted Christians. Jaghatai princes continued to be enthroned as Khans with diminishing powers over the rival groups of Moslem, Turkish and Mongol emirs, but these held all effective power and fought among themselves. After 1360 the Jaghatai Khans of Transoxiana were overthrown by Timur, a Mongol not descended from Chingis, who inaugurated a new age with his great empire. But since Timur directed his attacks against western Asia and India, and died before he could turn eastward to attack China, the House of Jaghatai survived for some time still in its eastern domains.

THE GOLDEN HORDE ON THE WESTERN STEPPES

On succeeding his father Jöchi as Khan of Kipchak in 1227, Batu took over an area that extended indefinitely westward from the Aral region into Eastern Europe. When he died, after the conquests described, he had made his western frontier a line that ran from the mouth of the Danube northward by the Carpathians to Kholm and Lublin and thence north-eastward to the Gulf of Finland and Lake Ladoga. His vaguely defined northern frontier lay along the edge of the forests until it joined the Upper Ob; his eastern frontier ran southward from the Ob across the Irtysh to the lower Syr Darya and Amu Darya; his southern frontier ran westward from the Amu Darya to the Caspian coast by the Kara Boghaz Göl and from its western coast south of the Terek and north of the Caucasus to the Black Sea. Not all of the territory was directly ruled. Beyond a line drawn from Nizhny Novgorod to a point south of Lwow were the territories of subject Russian princes: northern Khwarazm was often under a separate governor, and Caucasia was very loosely controlled. A certain suzerainty was exercised in Bulgaria also.

Batu's *ulus* thus embraced a large area of the fertile steppe most desired by nomads, but except in Khwarazm and in Russia it was without large towns or cultivated land. In this way it was like the *ulus* of Jaghatai and stood in contrast to the Yüan and Ilkhan realms. The large nomad element in the population from the beginning contained more Turks than Mongols, and its predominant language was Turkish, though Mongol was used for official purposes, as in the Khan's *yarlyks*. The nomads came eventually to be called Tartar by Russian and other writers, and it will be convenient to use this name henceforward for the Mongols in Russia. Batu and his successors kept their mobile *ordu* on the lower Volga, but a fixed capital was built at Old Sarai or Batu Sarai on the Volga, which was later replaced by New Sarai or Berke Sarai further up the river. These capitals were Tartar creations and depended on conditions maintained only under Tartar dominion.

The Asiatic territories were ruled by Batu's elder brother, Orda, and under him by other brothers, Shiban and Togha Temür, and afterwards by their descendants. They are little known except for their intervention in dynastic struggles in Russia. The Italian trading settlements in the Crimea at Kaffa, Sudak and Kertch continued to be maintained by the Genoese and Venetians. They enjoyed some independence in return for their services and contributed one element to the foreign population at Sarai. The Russian states subjugated by Batu were Smolensk, Chernigov, Seversk, Pereyaslavl, Murom, Ryazan and RostovSuzdal, in the east; in the west, Novgorod, Polotsk, Volhynia, Galicia, Kiev and Pinsk. Their princes had Tartar *darughachis* or *baskaks* at Court as political residents and collectors of tribute. The Tartars at first employed Moslems from Khwarazm as tax farmers, but replaced them because they were so hated.

The Tartars aimed at keeping the Russian princes disunited under supervision from the steppe. One of these always bore the title of Grand Duke, which could easily be revoked and transferred by the Khan. They continued their rivalries and quarrels as before. They and their boyars had interests which were different from those of their subject peasants and townsmen, and even stood to gain from Tartar rule if it was orderly and not too oppressive.

Resistance to the Tartars often came from the unprivileged classes. Relations with the Russian princes and with their rivals the Grand Dukes of Lithuania were of critical importance to the Tartars when they no longer drew any strength from their kinsmen in Asia.

Relations with the other Mongol powers were less important, except for the unceasing feud with the Ilkhans and later the invasion of Timur from former Jaghatai territory. From time to time the Tartar Khans co-operated with the Mameluk Sultans of Egypt against the Ilkhans.

After Batu died at Old Sarai about 1255 and his short-lived successors Sartakh and Ulagchi had also died, Berke, brother of Batu, succeeded in 1257 to the rule of the Golden Horde, as it is usually called after Batu's original gilded and gold-embroidered tent.

When he had been installed by Möngke, Berke sent his generals Burundai and Nogai to deal with the rising of Daniel of Galich and his son Lev in northern Russia. Their success was such that Pope Urban IV and the kings of Europe feared a new invasion. In 1263 the Russian Grand Duke Alexander Nevsky died. He had defeated the Teutonic Knights on Lake Ilmen, but had saved his people no less by enforcing strict obedience to the Tartars.

In the south Berke found himself at odds with Hülegü over the Caucasus, assigned by Möngke to Batu, and over the war against the Moslems, which he disliked because he had become a Moslem himself. After the battle of 'Ain Jalut, Baibars sought Berke's help against Hülegü. After the death of Möngke, Berke supported Arik Böge against Kubilai, so that he became the enemy of the Great Khan as well as of the Ilkhans, and was ready to ally himself with the Jaghatai Khans. He was the rival of Hülegü for influence with the Byzantines. In war against the Ilkhans, Berke's commander Nogai reached the Kura, but his troops retreated when Berke died in 1266. Berke left no son. Though Nogai was the ablest of the surviving Jöchids, the *kuriltai* chose Batu's grandson Möngke Temür, also a Moslem, to be Khan.

Möngke Temür made peace with the Ilkhans in 1268 against Baibars's wishes, but later he fell out with Abaka. When Abaka attacked the Mameluks in Syria, Baibars again asked for an alliance with the Golden Horde. Two large groupings of powers were formed for a short time: the Golden Horde and the Mame-luks joined forces with Venice, with Jacob of Sicily and with Alfonso of Aragon; the Ilkhans with the Genoese, with the Papacy, with Louis IX and with Charles of Anjou. In the Golden Horde Nogai remained the most powerful figure, controlling the Russian princes and urging them to fight the kingdom of Poland and the growing power of Lithuania. At the same time he set up two successive Tsars of Bulgaria, and gained great influence with the Byzantines. Baibars died in 1277, and his successor Kalawun was less hostile to the Ilkhans. Möngke Temür died in 1280 and was succeeded by his brother Tuda Möngke, who also became a Moslem in 1283.

For the next years the real ruler was still Nogai, who controlled the Russians and began a new advance into Hungary and southern Poland, where he made raids. Tuda Möngke, who had lost interest in affairs and had become a Sufi devotee, was forced to abdicate in favour of his nephew Teleböge. But Teleböge was so unsuccessful in war that Nogai had him seized and handed over to his rival Tokhta, son of Möngke Temür, who had him executed. Nogai then proclaimed Tokhta Khan with his three brothers. He himself took a special dominion in the Crimea based upon his own tribe, the Manghut. Thus there began to be two centres of Tartar power on the Russian steppe, a change which brought serious consequences.

Tokhta quarrelled with his brothers and was driven out. He took refuge with Nogai, who restored him as sole ruler. Once enthroned, Tokhta took the opposite side to Nogai in choosing a Grand Duke of Russia and in a war between Venice and Genoa.

In 1297 the two went to war themselves. In their first battle, on the Plate 39 Pruth, Nogai was victorious but did not manage to catch Tokhta. Two years later on the Kagamlyk Nogai was defeated and killed.

Tokhta had little difficulty in defeating Nogai's sons, not the equals of their father, and replaced them in the Crimea with two of his own. Like Abaka the Ilkhan, he took for one of his wives the illegitimate daughter of a Byzantine emperor. In the Caucasus he made the traditional demand for the country to be ceded, which was rejected by Ghazan in 1303. In his plan of attacking Öljeitü he failed to get the help of the Mameluk Sultan Al Malik al Nasir, who was occupied in resisting French crusaders; but when Öljeitü attacked, he beat him off. During a new rebellion of princes, which he sent his nephew Özbeg to suppress, Tokhta died at Sarai in 1312.

Tokhta was succeeded by Özbeg, a strong Moslem, who still obeyed the Yasa. Özbeg confirmed Ivan Kalita of Moscow, who had won a long struggle against the prince of Tver, as Grand Duke in 1328. Henceforward this office remained with the princes of Moscow, who finally freed Russia. In the west Özbeg checked the Lithuanians for a time in their bid to dominate Hungary and Poland and western Russia. In Caucasia he was himself checked by Abu Sa'id's general Choban and after the fall of the Ilkhans by Arpa. In 1341 he died at Sarai, and was succeeded by his son Janibeg.

Under Janibeg the Golden Horde began its long decline. Though he once took Tabriz and sent an army from Khwarazm into Khurasan, his main interest was in the west. In Russia, Grand Duke Simeon served him well, but he found it wise to confirm the ancient liberties of the Orthodox Church, especially as his opponent Casimir III of Poland threatened to end them in his dominions. Janibeg was also able to use Aligirdas, Grand Duke of Lithuania, to hold Casimir in check, and Simeon to hold back the Lithuanians. But the gainers in this balance of forces were the Ottoman Turks, whose power advanced north-ward through the Balkans, towards the Danube.

When Janibeg suddenly died in 1257 on his return from Azerbaijan, his son Berdibeg at once returned to Sarai to confirm his succession, abandoning the new conquests. The Golden Horde lost interest in the lands south of the Caucasus. Berdibeg was murdered in 1359, leaving great confusion. A succession of violent civil wars began both between Tartar rivals for the Khanate and between Russian princes, who attempted to throw off the yoke of Moscow and supported different Tartar pretenders. Meanwhile the Lithuanian Grand Dukes extended their power to the Dobrudja and the Dniestr and even to Kiev, but could not overcome the Grand Duke of Moscow. Finally the territory of the Golden Horde was divided between Mamai in the Crimea, Hajji Sarkis in Astrakhan and Urus Khan, who claimed to rule Khwarazm, in Sarai.

At this moment Timur of the Barlas tribe of Mongols, who was the equal of Chingis in warfare, made himself master of Trans-oxiana and Khwarazm in place of the Jaghatai Khans. At his court in Samarkand first Tokhtamysh, a nephew of Urus Khan, and then Edigü, a general of the Mangkut tribe, took refuge. Since Timur would not extradite them, Urus Khan prepared to attack Khwarazm, and Timur made ready to help his new vassal Tokhtamysh. But before the armies could meet, Urus Khan died in 1377, leaving Arabshah and other pretenders in Sarai. With Timur's help Tokhtamysh got possession of Astrakhan and Sarai in 1378. Meanwhile the Russian Grand Duke Dimitri, who had profited by the Tartar divisions, defeated Arabshah in 1378 on the Vozha in northern Ryazan, and went on to defeat Mamai in 1380 at Kulikovo Pole on the Upper Don. After this famous victory the Russians would have won in-dependence if the Tartars had remained disunited. But in another battle on the Kalka in 1381 Tokhtamysh in turn defeated Mamai, who escaped to Kaffa and was there murdered.

Tokhtamysh was not at once strong enough to compel the Russian princes to do homage. But in 1382 he took Moscow by capitulation. He then tried to renew ancestral ambitions by invading Caucasia and ravaging Transoxiana. Refugees, including Edigü, approached Timur, who turned northward from operations in Iran to attack Tokhtamysh. In 1391 Timur caught Tokhtamysh after a long pursuit on the Kandurcha near the Urals, and defeated him in a bloody battle.

Tokhtamysh was not yet overthrown, though other Khans were set up. In return for support from Vytautas of Lithuania he granted the latter's cousin Yagailo, now king of Poland, a *yarlyk* to govern and tax some Russian districts. He also granted Vassili of Moscow the rule of Nizhny Novgorod and some smaller principalities. But he received no help from the Ottomans or from the Mameluks, who were likewise threatened by Timur's advance. In 1394 Tokhtamysh again attacked Caucasia, but in 1395 his army was crushed on the Terek by Timur. Timur overran the lower Volga and advanced up the Don into Ryazan, where he stormed Yeletz, but he struck no further into Russia. Instead he destroyed the nomad base of Tokhtamysh's power by devastating Astrakhan, Sarai, Bulgar and the Crimea, before turning away to invade India. His operations drained the existing wealth of the Golden Horde and permanently weakened its control of cities and of the trade between Europe and India and China.

Tokhtamysh now depended absolutely on Vytautas of Lithuania, who hoped, by helping him, to dominate the territories of the Golden Horde. Tokhtamysh's rivals Temür Kutlugh and Edigü proclaimed themselves respectively Khan and emir and vassals of Timur. When Vytautas finally marched with some Russian allies to restore Tokhtamysh, his army met that of Edigü and Temür Kutlugh on the Vorskla in 1399. The Lithuanian force was completely destroyed, but Temür Kutlugh died of wounds. Tokhtamysh was killed later as a fugitive by a local Khan, Shadibeg. The Golden Horde thus maintained itself as an independent state, but under Edigü.

Edigü made no move against Lithuania but instead asked for Vytautas's help against Moscow. Vytautas refused, but did not help Moscow either, for he wished the Golden Horde and Moscow to weaken one another. Edigü then besieged Moscow without success. Within the Golden Horde, Tokhtamysh's sons, now supported by Moscow, fought rivals supported by Edigü, who was never himself Khan. Edigü's fortunes declined later, when Timur Khan son of Timur Kutlugh turned against him, followed by others. He tried to win support again from Vytautas, but was killed in a skirmish in 1418. When Vytautas eventually died in 1430, Lithuania was at once divided between pretenders. Moscow was once more the gainer, and the Golden Horde once more weakened by division.

The Golden Horde began to break up into independent hordes. In the west Ulugh Mahmed, cousin of Tokhtamysh, became Khan with Lithuanian support but had two rivals, Kepek and Devlet Berdi, sons of Tokhtamysh. More disturbance was created in 1422 by Barak, grandson of Urus Khan, who invaded from Kazakhstan and drove Ulugh Mahmed to take refuge with Vytautas. Devlet Berdi seized the Crimea about 1425. Other pretenders were Sa'id Ahmed, another son of Tokhtamysh, and Küchük Mahmed, grandson of Temür Kutlugh. Ulugh Mahmed had enough authority to confirm Vassili of Moscow as Grand Duke, but in 1437 was forced by his rivals to retreat to the Upper Oka, where Vassili then made war on him and his sons. Vassili was captured by the sons, but released on promise of an indemnity. Ulugh Mahmed's eldest son, Mahmudek, who wished to get this money himself, murdered his father. Mahmudek was proclaimed local Khan at Kazan in 1445. Vassili continued to rule Moscow, despite capture and blinding by his enemies.

Some Tartars from Ulugh Mahmed's horde joined Sa'id Ahmed, who now held the Crimea. Sa'id Ahmed was recognized in Moscow as Khan and received tribute. Mahmudek attacked him, but was defeated. Sa'id Ahmed, acting in support of Michael, a claimant to the Grand Duchy of Lithuania, invaded the Lithuanian dominion in 1449 taking Seversk and Kiev. In retaliation Casimir IV, King of Poland and Grand Duke of Lithuania, supported a rival Tartar prince Hajji Girai, who seized the Crimea in his turn and established a lasting dynasty there.

In 1449 Sa'id Ahmed sent a force to attack Moscow, but this was defeated. He had no more success either when he attacked in person in 1451 or later in 1459. When he invaded Podolia and Red Russia in 1452 he was taken in the rear by Hajji Girai. Vassili, dying in 1462, bequeathed his Grand Duchy to Ivan III without any reference to a Tartar overlord.

In the Crimea, Hajji Girai became so powerful that he laid claim to all the Kipchak territories, though Sa'id Ahmed and his sons were still active. When he died in 1466 the struggle for the succession went in favour of his ablest son, Mengli Girai. Meanwhile the Great Horde, as it was now called, revived its power under Küchük Mahmed's son Ahmed.

Though Ivan III of Moscow and Michael of Tver made an alliance against the Tartars, Ahmed first turned against Kiev, Volhynia and Podolia. But Casimir, who now distrusted the Crimean Khans, treated with him in 1471 for a joint attack on Moscow. Thus reassured, Ahmed attacked Moscow in 1472, but did not receive any help from Casimir, and had to retire and finally to make peace when his army was stricken with plague. In 1475 Ivan attacked Casimir for prompting Ahmed's invasion. He was assisted by Mengli Girai, who invaded Kiev and Podolia and demanded tribute. In 1476 Ahmed and his son Janibeg drove Mengli Girai to take refuge in Turkey with the Ottoman Sultan, who was now his ally. Ahmed again made war on Moscow, but had no success. In 1480 Ivan allied himself with Mengli Girai, now returned from Turkey, against Ahmed and

Casimir. When Ahmed once more marched on Moscow, Casimir failed him yet again. Mengli Girai and the Nogais then drove Ahmed eastward into Shibanid territory, where the Khan Aribeg attacked and killed him on the Donetz. The Great Horde was for a time without a leader.

In 1482 Ivan attacked Casimir in the north, while Mengli attacked him in Kiev and Podolia. The Lithuanians were also threatened by the Ottomans who advanced up the west coast of the Black Sea to Kilia and Akkerman. Casimir again applied for help to the Great Horde, which was now led by Ahmed's son Murteza and his brother Shaykh Ahmed. The Great Horde was defeated in 1485 by the Crimean Horde, Murteza was captured, but escaped. In 1487 Casimir, who had fallen out again with the Great Horde, fought it at Kopistryn and crushingly defeated it.

Ivan now allied himself with the Crimean Horde against the Great Horde, which he saw as his main enemy. Murteza, again at war with the Lithuanians, was defeated at Goryn and driven out by Shaykh Ahmed. Before Ivan and Mengli could attack the Great Horde and the Lithuanians, now again allied to it, Casimir died in 1492. His son Alexander, failing to win over Mengli, was attacked in 1493 by the Crimean Horde. But Mengli was stopped when the Great Horde attacked Perekop, cutting communications between the Crimea and Moscow. Ivan next made a treaty with Alexander for common action against the Tartars, but was still held back by his links with Mengli. Alexander and John of Poland on the other hand proposed to Shaykh Ahmed a joint attack on the Crimea Tartars, in which Mengli should be deposed. But their envoy was caught by Mengli. The Poles and Lithuanians now lost all influence in the south-east, largely because of their vacillating policies, so unlike the steady attitude of Moscow. They were cut off militarily when Mengli advanced to the Dniepr. The Ottomans thrust eastward from the Danube, and the Muscovites occupied the country to the north.

Against Mengli and Ivan, the Great Horde and the Polish–Lithuanian power were of little use to one another, for they had different interests and thus different main enemies. Shaykh Ahmed knew that a decisive conflict was coming with Mengli. He built a fortified camp by the confluence of the Sosna and the Don, but was deserted by his brother Sa'id Mahmed and by some of his troops, and was not supported by Alexander. In 1502 Mengli informed Ivan that he was ready to attack the Great Horde, now reduced to twenty thousand, at its camp by the mouth of the Desna. He did so, and finally destroyed Shaykh Ahmed's army. Shaykh Ahmed fled to Astrakhan and then, because he was rejected there, to Lithuania. Alexander, finding him now a mere embarrassment, executed him to improve relations with Mengli. Mengli now took Sarai. Thus the Great Horde came to an end in 1505. In this year Ivan III died and was succeeded by his son Ivan IV. The final triumph of Ivan IV over the Tartars outside the Crimea was largely due to his new weapons, cannon, large and small, and hand-guns, which were not known on the steppes.

But the Girai Khanate continued in the Crimea for a long time after this. The Crimean Tartars even took Moscow in 1571 and re-imposed tribute, which was paid to keep them quiet until the time of Peter the Great. Soon afterwards the State of Girai came to an end but its overlords, the Ottoman Sultans, remained suzerains of its territory until 1774, when they gave up this right by treaty to Catherine the Great. The Crimea was formally incorporated in Russia in 1783.

Plate 381

Material remains of the Golden Horde are best known from the few towns which were created by the Tartars themselves, such as Sarai Batu, Sarai Berke and Krym in the Crimea. Their wealth was due to trade and tribute and to the labours of workmen transported in war. Of these the best known from medieval description and modern excavation is Sarai Berke, believed to have had a population of more than a hundred thousand.

Sarai Berke was built without walls in the middle of a salt marsh. Part of the site was occupied by an artificial lake filled from the Volga. The river was also used, like the Orkhon at Karakorum, for reservoirs and water power. The Khan's residence was a great palace surmounted by the golden crescent of Islam. There were streets crowded with people, and five bazaars, but otherwise there was little room between the close-packed houses of wood or brick, which had no gardens. There were thirteen great mosques and many others. The inhabitants were Mongols, Alans, Kipchaks, Cherkesses, Russians, Byzantines, Italians and others, each nationality having its own bazaars. Visiting merchants and other subjects of foreign powers were accommodated in a special quarter surrounded by walls.

In one area, 450 metres square, excavators found the remains of bricks, pottery, plates, skins, textiles, weapons, tools, copper goblets and chandeliers, horse-trappings, tiles, nails and needles; also of fruits and vegetables, coffee, alum, salt-petre and other substances. These had all been damaged, but in some cases preserved, by the great sack and burning carried out by Timur's troops in his war against Tokhtamysh. The style of the durable remains such as pottery and architectural features was very much modelled on that of Khwarazm, though some Chinese, some Byzantine and some Mameluk influences are apparent.

Epilogue

THE TALE OF THE FAR-FLUNG activities of the imperial Mongols about Asia and Europe has been told. It remains to draw together the strands of Mongol history into some conclusion which shall still not extend into our own time. The tradition of conquest did not die among the Mongols without more serious attempts at revival than might have been expected from the confused and inglorious collapses of Chingisid rule in China, in Central Asia, in Iran and in Russia.

Among these attempts the empire of Timur cannot be included here. Though he and his immediate followers were of Mongol descent and were fully conscious of the tradition set by Chingis, Timur belongs mainly to another world. He founded his power largely at the expense of Chingisid princes, the last Jaghatai Khans of Transoxiana, and Tokhtamysh in the *ulus* of Jöchi. He spoke Turkish, like many other expatriate Mongols, and lived in Transoxiana, using Samarkand as his capital. From this centre, and not from Mongolia, he conquered his empire, and did so not as an enemy of Islam but as a professing and zealous Moslem, who promoted the faith in every way. Nor did he even seriously invade the eastern part of the *ulus* of Jaghatai, much less Mongolia, which remained unaffected by his wars.

For the conclusion of this history we return to Mongolia and the countries nearest to it, but some episodes will take us much further afield. The descendants of Chingis still have some share in these events.

After the fall of the Yüan in China, the first Ming emperors willingly accepted into their own armies Mongols who had surrendered or been captured. They even kept them as far as possible in the same units and under the same commanders, if these were not too high in rank or lineage. These Mongols, with their families, appear to have formed separate military communities wherever they were stationed. On the northern border special commanderies of partly immigrant Mongol soldiers were settled.

The immigrants came because of the impoverished and disordered state of Mongolia, where the Chingisid Khans began to lose their authority and local chiefs set themselves up as independent rulers, carrying on continual war. At the same time intervention by the Ming armies was always to be feared.

In 1372 Ayurshidara, son of Toghan Temür, was attacked by a Ming army in northern Mongolia, as Chin armies had attacked Mongol tribes before the rule of Chingis. Though this attack failed, the next Khan, Tokur Temür, was defeated heavily by a Chinese army of one hundred thousand south of Buyur Nor, after which he was put to death by one of his own kin. When his successor Elbek was defeated and killed by the Kirghiz Ugetchi in 1399 the continuous rule of Kubilai's line was interrupted. Ugetchi in turn fell before an alliance between the As or Alan chief Aruktai and Mahamu, chief of the Oïrat of western Mongolia. Aljai Temür, son of Elbek, tried to restore his family's fortunes, but foolishly refused to become a vassal of the Ming emperor Yang Lo, whose army then defeated him. Mahamu finally crushed him and became ruler of Mongolia in 1412. Thereafter the Oïrat were usually the dominant power in Mongolia: they were known as the Dörben Oïrat or Four Confederates, since they consisted of four tribes, the Choros, whose chiefs were paramount, the Dörböt, the Khochot and Törghüt. Mahamu established himself by becoming a vassal of the Ming, but still had rivals in Essekü, son of Ugetchi, in eastern Mongolia, and Adai, chief of the Korchin.

The Ming used the Oïrat to frustrate the attempts of the Chingisids to recover power. Toghon, son of Mahamu, did not seem immediately dangerous to them in his territory between Lake Baikal and the Irtysh when he attacked Vais, the Jaghatai Khan who ruled in the Ili valley and the Tarim basin. Under Toghon's son, Esen Taiji, the Oïrat empire reached its height, extending from Lake Balkash to Lake Baikal and thence to the Great Wall and southern Manchuria. In 1449 Esen Taiji defeated the emperor Ying tsung, killing more than 100,000 Chinese troops and taking the emperor prisoner, but he could not take Peking. He released the emperor in 1450 and made peace in 1453. His son Amasandji also overran the Jaghatai territory, but had to fight burdensome civil wars. In the west the Oïrat remained dominant, but in eastern Mongolia their power disappeared after Esen Taiji.

In the east, the line of Kubilai had not died out. Its fortunes were restored for the last time by Mandughai Khatun, widow of Mandughol Khan, the twenty-seventh successor of Chingis. She proclaimed Dayan, son of Mandughol's great-nephew, then five years old, as Khan. She brought him up, married him in 1481 when he was eighteen, and in 1491 led a successful campaign against the Oïrat. Dayan himself was a man of valour and energy. He reorganized the eastern Mongols in two groups: in one, the Chahar, the Khalka and the Uriangkat, in the other the Tümet and the Karachin. He made successful raids on China from Liaotung to Kansu during the years between 1497 and 1505, and reigned until 1543. But after his death his sons and grandsons divided the tribes among themselves according to Mongol custom, though the titular Khanate remained among the rulers of the Chahar. Altan Khan, who reigned from 1543 to 1583, campaigned successfully against the Ming through all their northern provinces, though he sought to trade with them too.

The Dayanid empire fell to pieces by the same process as the Chingisid, and more rapidly. The princes who drove the Oïrat westward and took their territory ceased to obey the Chahar Khans. The last paramount Khan, Ligdan, a notable warrior, was deposed in 1643 by the Manchus, after their leader Nurhachi had set up the Ch'ing dynasty in China. The Khans of the eastern Mongols became vassals of the Ch'ing.

In the west, the Oïrat, or Kalmuk as the Turks and Russians called them, again began an expansion in the sixteenth century as far as the Emba and the neighbourhood of Astrakhan, and further north in the territory of the last Shibanid Khans on the Tobol. They also raided the territory of Khiva in Transoxiana, They established friendly relations with the Russians, who hoped to use them against the nomads, Turkish or Turco-Mongol, who had once belonged to the Golden Horde. Of the Oïrat tribes, the Törghüt served the Russians for a time, but eventually became their enemies and returned to the Ili. The Khochot made them-selves dominant in Tibet as protectors of Buddhism, while the lamaistic Church educated the chiefs' sons from other Mongol tribes as well. The Choros drove them out of Tibet in 1717.

The Khans of the Choros created the Zungar realm on the Black Irtysh, the Urungu, the Imil and the Ili, maintaining contact with the Mongolian homeland and ruling also over the Dörböt and the Khoit. The most notable of their rulers was Galdan, who aimed at creating a new empire in Central Asia. He occupied not only Zungaria north of the Tien Shan but also Kashgaria to the south of the range, where he made an end of the last remnants of Jaghatai rule. He extended his territory to the Orkhon, the Tula and the Kerulen, evidently aiming to revive the greatness of Chingis. But he was defeated at Ulan Put'ong near Peking by Kang Hi, the great Ch'ing emperor, who now had artillery, made under the instruction of the Jesuits in his country. He attacked again in 1695, hoping to bring in the Korchin Mongols from northern Manchuria. But the Korchin kept the Chinese informed. Kang Hi's principal general, Fei Yang-ku, using artillery and musketry, crushed Galdan's force at Chao Modo near Urga, now Ulan-bator, in 1696. Kang Hi was preparing to drive the Zungars beyond the Tarbagatai when he heard that Galdan had died of an illness in 1697.

The eastern Mongols, who had been saved from Galdan, accepted Chinese political officers and an imperial garrison at

Urga. The Chinese allowed the Mongols in northern Mongolia and in the Ordos to keep their organization. Later Khans of the Zungars during the eighteenth century continued the struggle against the Chinese, until under the emperor Ch'ien-lung the Chinese conquered the Ili valley in 1757 and Kashgaria in 1758. Meanwhile the Russians had been extending their empire eastward across central Asia and Siberia to the Amur, where they came into collision with the Ch'ing, until a settlement was reached by the Treaty of Nerchinsk in 1685. Though the Ch'ing declined during the later eighteenth and nineteenth centuries, the Mongols were unable to gain much advantage, much less to revive their dominion, because of the power of Russia. They remained vassals of the Ch'ing until the dynasty fell in 1912.

The military power of the Mongols had been decisively reduced by fire-arms in the hands of their Russian and Chinese enemies, a development which had begun to be important during the fifteenth century. In their remote territories in the northern parts of Inner Asia they had not been able to get or to make the new weapons. In this respect they were much less fortunate than the kindred Ottoman Turks, who at the very time when the Golden Horde was losing its power became the greatest military power in western Asia and eastern Europe.

Another cause for their loss of military power has been seen in their conversion to the lamaistic Buddhism of the Yellow Church of Tibet. Many of them became lamas instead of warriors. It is symbolic that the site of Karakorum was later occupied by the lamasery of Erdeni Tzu, founded in 1586 and for some centuries the chief centre of Buddhism in Mongolia.

This, then, is the story of the Mongols down to the time of their disappearance as an independent power before the pressure of the last Chinese dynasty and of the new Russian Empire in the Far East, which caught them, as they had never before been caught, between two advancing fronts. This is also the end of northern

nomads' power as a danger to settled civilization. The effects
on the Mongols of the fall of the Ch'ing Dynasty, of the communist revolution in Russia, and now of the communist revolution in China, fall beyond the limits of this book.

Gibbon, who has much to say on the merits of the Mongols,
also justifies his attention to them and earlier nomads by saying:
'Nor can I refuse myself to those events which from their un-
common magnitude will interest a philosophic mind in the
history of blood.' The history of the nomads has always been
bloody, and never more so than in the age of the Mongols, who
are remembered chiefly for their massacres and devastations. But
the victories which they used in this manner were won by an
unequalled hardihood and discipline, with numbers which
study has shown to have been much smaller than those of most
of the armies that they faced. They also had two commanders
who as strategists and tacticians were unsurpassed in history:
Chingis Khan, and Sübüdei. Their conquests were barbarian
invasions, but not, like other such events, comparable to natural
catastrophes. The nearest analogy to their achievement is in the
victorious spread of Islam, also the work of nomad armies with a
fanatical discipline and devotion. But the conquering Arabs
had a religion which created a distinctive civilization, one which
the Mongols themselves could not destroy, and which has long
survived the days of Mongol power. The mission of Chingis
and his house was not comparable to that of Islam, and the
Mongols could found no new epoch of civilization. The Mongols
of our own day have not forgotten the power of their ancestors,
but they have other interests and do not wish to be regarded as
men of blood.

Genealogical Tables

I THE HOUSE OF CHINGIS KHAN

Great Khans with the title Khan after their names

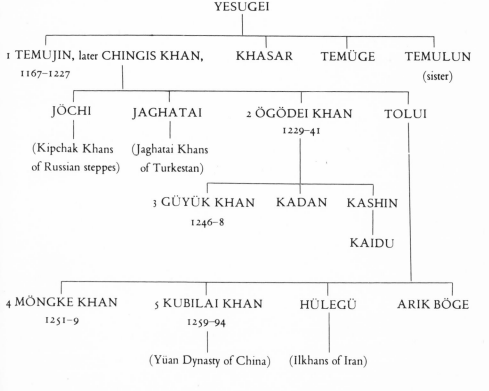

II THE HOUSE OF KUBILAI
(YÜAN DYNASTY OF CHINA)

*Mongol names given first, where known, then Buddhist names,
then Chinese temple-names (posthumous)*

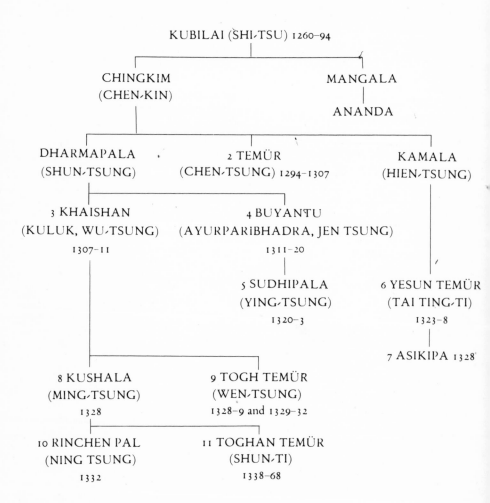

KUBILAI (SHI-TSU) 1260–94

CHINGKIM
(CHEN-KIN)

MANGALA

ANANDA

DHARMAPALA
(SHUN-TSUNG)

2 TEMÜR
(CHEN-TSUNG) 1294–1307

KAMALA
(HIEN-TSUNG)

3 KHAISHAN
(KULUK, WU-TSUNG)
1307–11

4 BUYANTU
(AYURPARIBHADRA, JEN TSUNG)
1311–20

5 SUDHIPALA
(YING-TSUNG)
1320–3

6 YESUN TEMÜR
(TAI TING-TI)
1323–8

7 ASIKIPA 1328

8 KUSHALA
(MING-TSUNG)
1328

9 TOGH TEMÜR
(WEN-TSUNG)
1328–9 and 1329–32

10 RINCHEN PAL
(NING TSUNG)
1332

11 TOGHAN TEMÜR
(SHUN-TI)
1338–68

III THE ILKHANS OF IRAN

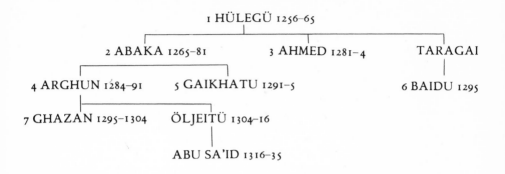

1 HÜLEGÜ 1256–65

2 ABAKA 1265–81   3 AHMED 1281–4   TARAGAI

4 ARGHUN 1284–91   5 GAIKHATU 1291–5   6 BAIDU 1295

7 GHAZAN 1295–1304   ÖLJEITÜ 1304–16

ABU SA'ID 1316–35

IV THE HOUSE OF JAGHATAI IN TURKESTAN

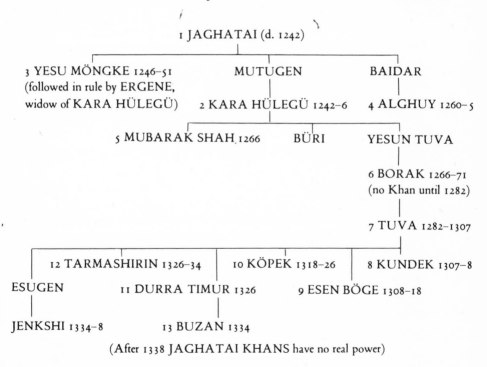

1 JAGHATAI (d. 1242)

3 YESU MÖNGKE 1246–51   MUTUGEN   BAIDAR
(followed in rule by ERGENE,
widow of KARA HÜLEGÜ)   2 KARA HÜLEGÜ 1242–6   4 ALGHUY 1260–5

5 MUBARAK SHAH 1266   BÜRI   YESUN TUVA

6 BORAK 1266–71
(no Khan until 1282)

7 TUVA 1282–1307

12 TARMASHIRIN 1326–34   10 KÖPEK 1318–26   8 KUNDEK 1307–8

ESUGEN   11 DURRA TIMUR 1326   9 ESEN BÖGE 1308–18

JENKSHI 1334–8   13 BUZAN 1334

(After 1338 JAGHATAI KHANS have no real power)

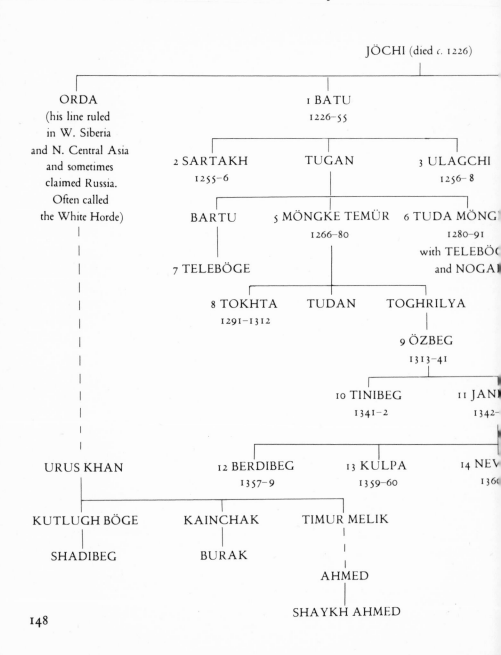

JÖCHI (died *c.* 1226)

ORDA
(his line ruled
in W. Siberia
and N. Central Asia
and sometimes
claimed Russia.
Often called
the White Horde)

1 BATU
1226–55

2 SARTAKH
1255–6

TUGAN

3 ULAGCHI
1256–8

BARTU

5 MÖNGKE TEMÜR
1266–80

6 TUDA MÖNG
1280–91
with TELEBÖ(
and NOGAI

7 TELEBÖGE

8 TOKHTA
1291–1312

TUDAN

TOGHRILYA

9 ÖZBEG
1313–41

10 TINIBEG
1341–2

11 JAN

URUS KHAN

12 BERDIBEG
1357–9

13 KULPA
1359–60

14 NEV
136(

KUTLUGH BÖGE

KAINCHAK

TIMUR MELIK

SHADIBEG

BURAK

AHMED

SHAYKH AHMED

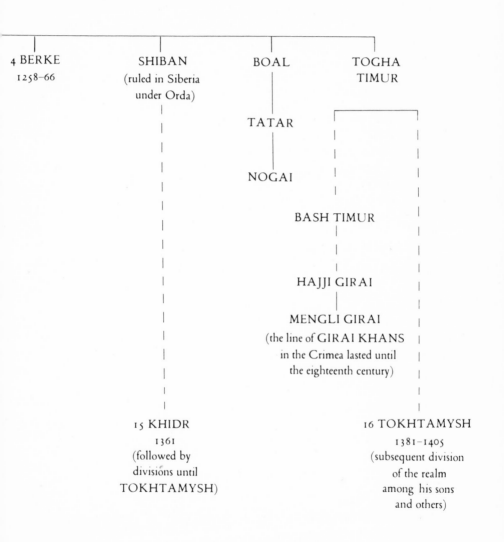

4 BERKE	SHIBAN	BOAL	TOGHA
1258–66	(ruled in Siberia under Orda)		TIMUR

TATAR

NOGAI

BASH TIMUR

HAJJI GIRAI

MENGLI GIRAI
(the line of GIRAI KHANS
in the Crimea lasted until
the eighteenth century)

15 KHIDR	16 TOKHTAMYSH
1361	1381–1405
(followed by	(subsequent division
divisions until	of the realm
TOKHTAMYSH)	among his sons
	and others)

*Reigning Khans of the united Golden Horde are numbered and dated
but Khans not descended from Batu are not, except for Tokhtamysh*

Notes on the Text

INTRODUCTION

1 For this suggestion, *see* P. Poucha, *Die Geheime Geschichte der Mongolen*, 191. The questions arising over the transmission of the *Secret History* in Mongol and in Chinese and over the scripts used for the Mongol original continue to be debated, as in Haenisch's edition and translation and in Poucha's monograph here mentioned, in Wei Kwei-Sun's translation of the *Yuan Chao Pi Shi* and in Kuo Yi Pao, *Studies on the Secret History of the Mongols*, 1965, all of which have bibliographies.

2 The *Altan Debter* is discussed by Pelliot and Hambis, *Histoire des Campagnes de Genghis Khan* and in Poucha, *op. cit.* 15 ff. It will no doubt be treated by Boyle in his forthcoming translation of Rashid's *History of the Tribes*, which is based on the same material, whether or not Rashid actually studied the *Altan Debter*.

3 The *Altan Tobchi* contains many passages from the *Secret History* and much added Buddhist matter. It is dated somewhere in the period 1649–1736. *See* F. W. Cleaves *Altan Tobchi: A Brief History of the Mongols*, which includes a Foreword by Cleaves and a Preface by A. Mostaert, and Poucha, *op. cit.,* 9 ff.

4 Besides Schmidt's edition and translation, now reprinted, which is mentioned in the Bibliography, there is the new English translation by John R. Krueger, *Sagang Sechen: History of the Eastern Mongols* (occasional Papers of the Mongolic Society No. 2, 1967, Part I, which ends at 1399. Part II is promised shortly).

5 Fragments of the Yasa, preserved in various languages, are translated and discussed in V. A. Riasonovsky, *Fundamental Principles of Mongol Law* (Tientsin 1937). See also G. Vernadsky, 'The Scope and Content of Chingis Khan's Yasa'. (*Harvard Journal of Asiatic Studies* 3 (1938), 337–60.)

6 See Riasonovsky, *op. cit.,* 86–91.

7 Among articles or books dealing with such documents a few may be mentioned. On Mongol documents or inscriptions originating in Mongolia: S. Murayama, 'Uber die Inschrift auf dem Stein des Čingis'

(*Oriens* III (1956), 108–12). P. Pelliot, 'Les Mongols et la Papauté, 22–25, on the letter of Güyük in 1246 to Innocent IV, and on the same subject and similar ones, A. Mostaert and F. W. Cleaves, 'Trois documents mongols des Archives Secrètes Vaticanes' (*HJAS* 15 (1952), 419–506; Appendix II, 485–95).

On inscriptions found in China: Yöngsiyebü Rinčen, 'L'inscription sino-mongole de la stèle de Möngke Gayan' (*Central Asiatic Journal* 4 (1958), 130–42); F. W. Cleaves, 'The Sino-Mongolian inscription of 1362 in Memory of Prince Hindu' (*HJAS* 12 (1949), 1–133); 'The Sino-Mongolian Inscription of 1335 in Memory of Chang Ying-Jui' (*HJAS* 13 (1950), 1–131); 'The Sino-Mongolian inscription of 1338 in Memory of Jiguntei' (*HJAS* 14 (1951), 1–104, and 'The Sino-Mongolian inscription of 1346' (*HJAS* 15 (1952), 1–123).

On documents originating in Iran: E. Haenisch, 'Zu den Briefen der Mongolischen Khane Argun und Äljeitü an den König Philipp den Schönen von Frankreich 1289 und 1305' (*Oriens* II (1949), 216–235). A. Mostaert and F. W. Cleaves, *Les Lettres de 1289 et 1305 des Ilkhan Aryun et Öljeitü à Philippe le Bel,* 1962 (Complete edition); F. W. Cleaves, 'The Mongolian Documents in the Musée de Teheran' (*HJAS* 16 (1953), 1–107).

On documents from Russia: I. N. Berezin, *Khanskie Yarlyki* (Yarlyks of the Khans), 3 vols., 1050–51, and books and articles mentioned in Spuler, *Die Goldene Horde,* 456–458.

8 The Chinese sources for the various events of Mongol invasion and rule of China are carefully indicated in the relevant notes to Vol. V of Franke's *Geschichte des Chinesischen Reiches.* They are not easily accessible in the original and translations are few and incomplete, so that Franke's close summary in the narrative of Vol. IV is invaluable when it is read in conjunction with the notes of Vol. V. The *Liao-shi, Chin-shi* and *Sung-shi* were put together quickly in 1344–45 under the last Yüan emperor, Toghan Timur, by twenty-four scholars under the Mongol minister Tokto from earlier sources. The *Yüan shi* was composed under the Ming Dynasty. For a general account, *see* Franke *op. cit.* IV, 1–9. A few more details will be given in the notes to the chapter on the Yüan Dynasty.

9 Ibn al Athir's work is the *Kamil fi al Tawarikh,* literally 'The Complete in Histories', and extends down to 1231. It was edited by C. H. Tornberg

in 14 volumes under the title *Ibn al Athiri Chronicon* (1851–1876) and translated in part by J. T. Reinaud and C. F. Defrémery in *Recueil des Historiens des Croisades: Historiens Orientaux* under the title *Extraits de la Chronique Kamel Altewarykh* (1872–87).

10 Yakut al Hamawi, or al Rumi, was of Byzantine origin. His work, the *Mudjairs al Buldan*, was edited by G. Wüstenfeld under the title *Jacuts geographisches Wörterbuch* in 1866–73. It is a dictionary of mixed historical and geographical information. Yakut fled from Khwarazm to escape the Mongols.

11 Muhammad al Nasawi's work is called *Sirat al Sultan Djalal-al-Din Mankabirti*. It was edited by O. Houdas in 1891 and translated by him in 1895 under the title *Histoire du Sultan Djelal-ad-Din Mankabirti, Prince du Kharezm*.

12 For Juvaini's work, *see* the edition by J. A. Boyle mentioned in the Bibliography.

13 There is no complete translation of Rashid in any western language even in Russian, where I. N. Berezin in the years 1858–68 translated only the parts covering the history of the tribes and the career of Chingis. But a new translation, *Rashid-ad-Din, Sbornik Letopisei,* by various hands, has been in progress since 1952 and should soon be finished. For the work of Quatremère and Boyle, *see* the Bibliography.

14 Wassaf's *Tazjzi at al Amsar wa Tasdji at al Asar* literally 'Division of the towns and propulsion of the centuries' covers the years 1257–1328. A translation was begun by J. von Hammer but never went beyond the first volume published in 1850.

15 Juzjani's *Tabakat-i-Nasri* was printed in *Bibliotheca Indica* in 1864 and translated in the same series by Raverty in 1873–76.

16 Mirkhond's *Rawdat al Safc (Garden of Purity)* was a compilation of universal history and was continued in more original fashion by his grandson Khondemir (Khwandamir). There are partial translations by various authors but no complete version exists.

17 Abu'l Ghazi (1603–63) reigned for 23 years as Khan of Khwarazm. His work was translated by Desmaisons under the title *Histoire des Mongols et des Tatares*.

18 Bar Hebraeus (1226–86) was the son of a Jewish physician and himself a physician. His *Syrian Chronicle* uses the Persian history of Shams-ad-

Din Sahib Diwan, brother of Djuvaini and like him a minister for the Mongol period. His work is translated in Sir E. A. Wallis Budge, *The Chronography of Gregory Abu'l Faraj . . . translated from the Syriac* (1932).

19 *See* Sir E. A. W. Budge, *The Monks of Kublai Khan, Emperor of China* (1928).

20 *See* R. P. Blake and R. N. Frye, *History of the Nation of Archers (The Mongols) by Grigor of Akanc'*, hitherto ascribed to Magak the Monk (*HJAS* 12 (1949), 269–399). Also from Armenia are the reports of Kirakos of Ganjak and Vartan for which *see* E. Dulaurier, 'Les Mongols d'après les historiens Arméniens' (*Journal Asiatique* 1858 I, 195–255, 426–73, 481–508, 1860; II, 273–322).

21 In *Recueil des Historiens des Croisades. Documents Armeniens II* (1906), 115–363.

22 Published by Assemani in *Bibliotheca Orientalis,* Vol. III, Part 2, 500. This Sampad was brother of King Hayton. The historian Hayton is a different man from King Hayton, though a kinsman.

23 *See* n. 20. Most of this material is also in G. Altunian, *Die Mongolen und ihre Eroberungen in Kaukasischen und Kleinasiatischen Ländern im XIII Jahrhundert* (1911).

24 These, along with Chalkokondyles, Dukas and Nikephoros Gregoras, are to be found in the various volumes of the *Corpus Scriptorum Historiae*, edited by Schopen, Bekker and others, but have not been translated into any western language.

25 They are very seldom translated into any western language. For lists of them see Vernadsky, *The Mongols and Russia,* 409–10 and Spuler, *Die Goldene Horde,* 477–78.

26 The *Speculum Historiale* of Vincent de Beauvais is part of his encyclopedia, the *Speculum Maius*, completed in 1253 and first printed at Douai in 1624 by the Benedictines. Most of his information about the Mongols came from Simon de Saint Quentin's *Historia Tartarorum*, which he quotes extensively in combination with Carpini's account. *See* J. Richard, *Simon de Saint Quentin, Histoire des Tartares* (1965). The *Chronica Majora* of Matthew of Paris, ending in 1259, was edited by Luard in 1853. Guillaume de Nangis' Chronicle is in the *Recueil des Historiens des Croisades*, and Salimbene's in *Monumenta Germaniae Historica Scriptorum Tormus* XXXII (1905–13). These are not translated. On these writers *see* P. Pelliot, 'Les Mongols et la Papauté' (*Revue de*

l'Orient Chrétien XXIII (1922), 3–30; XXIV (1924), 225–335; XXVII (1931), 3–84).

27 The original Latin of Carpini is edited by A. van den Wyngaert in *Itinera et relationes fratrum minorum saeculorum* XIII and XIV (*Sinica Franciscana* I) 1929, 3–130.

28 For the original *see* van den Wyngaert, *op. cit.*, 335–355.

29 For the original *see* van den Wyngaert, *op. cit.*, 147–332.

30 *See* G. D. Painter, *The Tartar Relation*, 54–101, for Latin text and translation.

31 The oldest version is the French text, for which see the edition of L. F. Benedetto, *Il Milione*, with Italian introduction (1928). The medieval Italian version has been edited by D. Olivieri, *Il Milione seconda il testo della 'Crusca' reintegrata con gli altri codici italiani* (1928). The medieval Latin version is reprinted from the manuscript of Toledo as Vol. II in Moule-Pelliot.

32 For Odoric, *see* Sir Henry Yule, *Cathay and the Way Thither* (Hakluyt Society 1913, Vol. I, 1–162; Vol. II, Appendix on pp. 1–420); also C. H. A. Schaefer and H. Cordier *Les Voyages en Asie au XIVe siècle du bienheureux frère Odoric de Pordenone* (1882). The Latin MS. is in MSS. Lat. 2884 of *c.* 1350 in the Bibliothèque Nationale.

33 For evidence of this type see the chapters dealing with the Mongol Empire and its successor-states, and the notes to them. The date of the *Secret History* has been reconsidered by Igor de Rachewilz, 'Some Remarks on the Dating of the *Secret History of the Mongols*', *Monumenta Serica* XXIV (1965) 185–203. He argues that the main text, 1–268, which deals with the ancestry and life of Chingis Khan, was composed within one year of Chingis' death in 1227 and recited with ceremony at the *kuriltai* on the Kerulen which chose his successor. The title *Mongol-Un Niucha Tobcha'an* could not have belonged to this original version, which should rather be called, after its first words, *Činggis-Qahan-U Hujaur* (The Origin of Chingis Khan).

CHAPTER I

1 Details of the Mongol mode of life as given by Carpini, Rubruck and Marco Polo are supplemented from E. Huc, *Souvenirs of a Journey through Tartary, Tibet and China,* first published in French in 1852, newly

edited by J./M. Planchet and translated in 1931, and O. Lattimore, 'The Geographical Factor in Mongol History' (*The Geographical Journal* XCI No. 1, January 1938) reprinted in *Studies in Frontier History*, 241 ff.

CHAPTER III

1 On the relations between the Popes and the Great Khans, *see* particu/ larly P. Pelliot, 'Les Mongols et la Papauté' (*Revue de l'Orient Chrétien* XXIII (1923), 3–33; XXIV (1924), 225–235; XXVIII (1931), 3–84); also *Simon de Saint Quentin: Histoire des Tartares*, edited by J. Richard; and Painter, *The Tartar Relation* (*see* Bibliography). The original Latin of Carpini and Rubruck is edited by A. van den Wyngaert in *Sinica Franciscana* I. *Itinera et relationes Fratrum Minorum saeculorum* XIII and XIV (1929), which has other material too.

2 For the excavations on the site of Karakorum, *see* S. V. Kiselev and others, *Drevnemongolskie Goroda (Ancient Mongol Towns)*, Moscow 1965, of which no part, so far as I know, has been translated or summarized in any western language. The relevant parts are 'Iz Istorii Kara/Koruma' (From the History of Karakorum) a historical sketch by S. V. Kiselev and I. Ya. Merpert; 'Dvoretz Kara/Koruma' (The Palace of Kara/ korum) by S. V. Kiselev and L. A. Evtiukhova; and 'Phreski naiden/ niye pod Dvortzom Ugedeya v Kara/Koruma' (Frescoes that came to light under the Palace of Ögödei at Karakorum), mainly on pre/ Mongol material of Buddhist origin.

3 On the Chinese invention of white cast iron, *see* L. Aitchison, *A History of Metals* Vol. I, 236, where it is dated to the first century or the Christian era. For details of the Chinese mechanical bellows driven by water/ wheel, such as must have been used at Karakorum in Mongol service, *see* J. Needham, *Science and Civilization in China*, Vol. 4, Part 2, Section 27 (1965), 369, 'The Metallurgical Blowing/Engines of the Han and Sung', where in Figs. 602 and 603 a blowing/engine is illustrated. It consists of a horizontal water/wheel with paddle/shaped spokes set on a vertical shaft and driven by a sloping race of water. On the same shaft is a driving wheel connected by a crossed belt with a pulley. On the same shaft with the pulley is a crank which drives a connecting rod and piston/rod back and forth to draw open and push closed the boards of a

fan bellows. At Karakorum the water must have been drawn from the river at some point upstream high enough for it to make a race as it descended.

CHAPTER IV

YÜAN

1 On Kubilai's invasion of Japan, *see* A. Pfitzmaier, 'Die Geschichte der Mongolen Angriffe auf Japan' (*Sitzungsber. der Wiener Akadamie der Wiss.* LXXVI (1874), 105–200, and K. Enoki, 'Marco Polo and Japan' in *Oriente Poliano.*

2 On Kubilai's use of foreigners in China, *see* Ch'en Yüan, *Western and Central Asians in China under the Mongols,* 1966.

3 On Phagspa and his script, *see* N. Poppe, *The Mongolian monuments in P'hags-pa script.* Second edition, translated and edited by J. R. Krueger, *Göttinger Asiatische Forschungen* VIII (1957).

4 On Kubilai's paper money, *see* H. Franke, *Geld und Wirtschaft in China unter der Mongolenherrschaft. Beiträge zur Wirtschaftsgeschichte der Yüan-Zeit* (1949).

THE ILKHANS

5 On the Ilkhans' relations with European powers, *see* A. Mostaert and F. W. Cleaves, *Les Lettres de 1289 et 1305 des Ilkhan Aryun et Öljeitü à Philippe le Bel,* 1962, with Mongol texts translations and commentaries.

Bibliography

BARTOLD, V. V. *Turkestan down to the Mongol Invasions.* London 1928.

BRETSCHNEIDER, E. *Medieval Researches from Eastern Asiatic Sources.* Second ed. London 1910. 2 vols. Reprinted New York 1966.

D'OHSSON, BARON A. C. M. *Histoire des Mongols depuis Tchinguiz-khan jusqu'à Timour Bey ou Tamerlan.* Second impression, Amsterdam 1852. 4 vols.

FRANKE, O. *Geschichte des Chinesischen Reiches.* Berlin 1948. 5 vols.

GROUSSET, R. *L'Empire des Steppes.* Paris 1939.

— *L'Empire Mongol.* Paris 1941.

l'Extrème Orient. Paris 1929. 2 vols.

SPULER, B. *Geschichte der Islamischen Länder.* Second ed., *Die Mongolen-zeit.* Leiden 1953.

— *Geschichte Mittelasiens seit dem Auftreten der Türken* in *Geschichte Mittelasiens.* Handbuch des Orientalistik, V. Leiden 1966.

VERNADSKY, G. *The Mongols and Russia.* Yale 1959.

YULE, SIR HENRY. *Cathay and the Way Thither.* New ed. by H. Cordier. London, Hakluyt Society, and New York 1914–16. 4 vols.

See notes on the sources in all books mentioned in the General Bibliography, and also in:

SPULER, B. *Die Mongolen in Iran.* Berlin 1955.

— *Die Goldene Horde : die Mongolen in Russland.* Second ed., enlarged. Wiesbaden 1965.

Also the following editions or translations of sources:

BARTOLD, V. V. *Four Studies on the History of Central Asia.* Leiden 1962.

BEAZLEY, C. R. *The Texts and Versions of John de Plano Carpini and William de Rubruquis,* as printed for the first time by Hakluyt in 1598, together with some shorter pieces. London, Hakluyt Society, 1903.

BOYLE, J. A. *Ata Malik Juvaini. The History of the World-Conqueror.* Manchester 1958. 2 vols.

CLEAVES, F. W. *The Secret History of the Mongols.* Harvard 1960.

GROUSSET, R. *L'Empire des Steppes.* Paris 1939.

HAENISCH, E. *Die Geheime Geschichte der Mongolen.* Second ed., revised. Leipzig 1948.

HEISSIG, W. *A Lost Civilisation: the Mongols Rediscovered.* Translated by D. J. S. Thomson. London and New York 1966.

KRADER, L. *Social Organisation of the Mongol-Turkic Pastoral Nomads.* The Hague and New York 1963.

MOULE, A. C. and PELLIOT, P. *Marco Polo. The Description of the World.* Translation in 2 vols. London 1938.

— *Notes on Marco Polo.* Paris 1959–63. 2 vols, in same format.

PAINTER, G. D. *The Tartar Relation,* edited with introduction, translation and commentary, in Skelton, R. A., Marston, T. E. and Painter, G. D., *The Vinland Map and the Tartar Relation.* Yale 1965.

PELLIOT, P. and HAMBIS, L. *Histoire des Campagnes de Gengis Khan.* Leiden 1951. (Chinese version of material from the *Altan Debter.*)

QUATREMÈRE, M. *Histoire des Mongols de Perse I.* Paris 1836. (Rashid on the conquests of Hülegü. All that was ever published of this edition of Rashid.)

RISCH, F. *Johann de Plano Carpini. Geschichte der Mongolen und Reisebericht 1245–1247.* Leipzig 1930.

— *Wilhelm von Rubruck. Reise zu den Mongolen 1253– 1934.* Leipzig

ROCKHILL, W. W. *The Journey of William of Rubruck to the Eastern Parts of the World 1253–55,* as narrated by himself, with two accounts of the earlier journey of John of Plan de Carpini. London, Hakluyt Society, 1900.

SCHMIDT, I. J. *Geschichte der Ost-Mongolen und ihres Fürstenhauses.* Verfasst von Ssanang Ssetsen Chungtaidschi. St Peterburg 1829.

WALEY, ARTHUR. *The Secret History of the Mongols.* London 1963, New York 1964. (Translation of certain passages only on pp. 217–291.)

WEI KWEI-SUN. *The Secret History of the Mongol Dynasty (Yuan Chao Pi Shi).* Muslim University, Aligarh 1957.

YULE, SIR HENRY and CORDIER, H. *The Book of Ser Marco Polo the Venetian Concerning the Kingdoms and Marvels of the East.* Third ed. London 1903–63.

On the general history of nomadism:
PHILLIPS, E. D.   *The Royal Hordes*. London and New York 1965.

On Mongolia and the relations of nomads with the Chinese:
LATTIMORE, O.   *The Inner Asian Frontiers of China*. (Reprint.) Boston 1962.
— *Studies in Frontier History. Collected Papers 1928–1958*. London and New York 1962.
FRANKE, O.   *op. cit.* Vol. I.

On the Hsiung Nu:
WATSON, BURTON.   *Records of the Grand Historian of China, translated from the Shih chi of Ssu Ma-chien*. New York 1961. Vol. II, pp. 155–92.

On the Turks:
BARTOLD, V. V.   *Histoire des Turcs d'Asie Centrale*. Paris 1945.

On Mongol institutions:
VLADIMIRTSOV, B.   *Le Régime Social des Mongols*. Paris 1948.

On the rise of Chingis Khan:
The Secret History of the Mongols in the editions mentioned.
MARTIN, H. D.   *The Rise of Chingis Khan and his Conquest of North China*. Baltimore 1950.
POUCHA, PAVEL.   *Die Geheime Geschichte der Mongolen als Geschichts-quelle und Literaturdenkmal. Archiv Orientalni*. Supplementa IV (1956), Prague 1956.

On Chingis Khan's eastern wars:
FRANKE, O.   *op. cit.* Vols. IV and V.
MARTIN, H. D.   *op. cit.*

On his western wars:
BARTOLD, V. V.   *Turkestan down to the Mongol Invasion*. London 1928.
Personal details of Chingis's life are repeated through studies and biographies that are written from time to time such as:
PRAVDIN, M.   *The Mongol Empire. Its Rise and Legacy*. London 1940.

On the Great Khans:
The works already mentioned of d'Ohsson, Howorth, Grousset and Spuler; early chapters of Vernadsky, *The Mongols and Russia,* Franke, *Geschichte des Chinesischen Reiches,* vols IV and V, Boyle, *Juvaini,* Quatremère, *Histoire des Mongols de Perse,* and the editions of Carpini, Rubruck and Marco Polo.

OLSCHKI, P. *Marco Polo's Asia.* An Introduction to his Description of the World called Il Milione. Translated by J. A. Scott and revised by the author. Berkeley and Los Angeles 1960.

ORIENTE POLIANO. *Studi e conferenze tenute all' Istituto Italiano per il medio e estremo Oriente.* Rome 1958. A collection of papers by various authors.

Kubilai and the Yüan Dynasty:
FRANKE. *op. cit.* Vols. IV and V.
SERRUYS, H. *The Mongols in China during the Hung-Wu Period 1368–1398.* Brussels 1959.

The Ilkhans:
BROWNE, E. G. *A Literary History of Persia.* Vol III. *The Tartar Dominion, 1256–1502.* Cambridge 1928.
Handbuch der Orientalistik. Geschichte der Islamischen Länder: Zweiter Abschnitt. Die Mongolenzeit. Leiden 1953.
SPULER, B. *Die Mongolen in Iran.* Berlin 1955.

The House of Jaghatai:
BARTOLD, V. V. *Four Studies on the History of Central Asia.* Vol. I, containing a *Short History of Turkestan* and *History of the Semirechye.* Translated by V. and T. Minorsky. Leiden and New York 1962.

The Golden Horde:
GREKOV, B. and IAKOUBOVSKI, A. *La Horde d'Or et la Russie.* Paris 1961.
SPULER, B. *Die Goldene Horde. Die Mongolen in Russland 1223–1502.* Wiesbaden 1965.
VERNADSKY, G. *The Mongols and Russia.* Yale 1959.

1

3

7

8

9

10

11

12

14

15

6

7

20, 21

22

23

24

25

les celegoit coinacenu
fu q feiffent defenes tos
ceaus qui poient armes
porter. Et ordena q fur
chascune defene fult un

names celas cuas qui
chascu amenast son aine
filz deuat soi. 7 quat il
orét ce fait lors comēta
q chascu copast la teste ce

26, 27

28

29

31

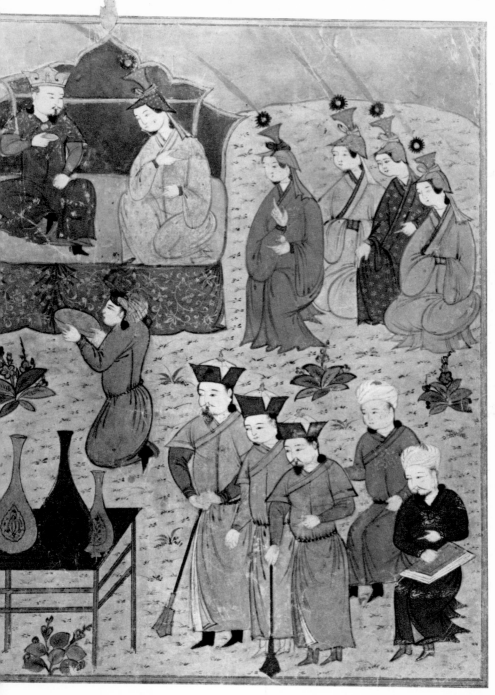

33

35

皇元敕賜大司徒龍禪軍□岳多昌公止碑

36

a

b

c

d

e

f

g

h

i

j

k

l

39

Notes on the Plates

1 Chinese miniature representing a Mongol horseman with game killed. The horseman's dress, weapons and gear are accurately shown, particularly his bowcase which can also hold arrows. For hunting, no armour is worn and the only weapon used is the bow and arrow. The short-legged, stocky Mongolian pony and its harness are well rendered. Courtesy Musée Guimet, Paris.

2 Portrait of Chingis Khan in the Imperial Portrait Gallery, Peking. This portrait is more a conventional notion of Chingis than an accurate likeness, but it is probably nearer the reality than others. It shows his red hair, an indication of some white ancestry in his family.

3 Temujin, enthroned, has himself proclaimed Chingis Khan. On the right are his sons Ögödei and Jöchi. From illuminated Persian MS. of Rashid-ad-Din. MS. Suppl. Persan 1113, folio 44 verso. Courtesy Bibliothèque Nationale, Paris.

4 Chingis Khan enthroned with Börtei, while his sons kneel before him, courtiers stand about, and a meal is prepared. Note the *boktag* headdress worn by Börtei. MS Suppl. Persan 1113, folio 126 verso. Courtesy Bibliothèque Nationale, Paris.

5 Chingis Khan, enthroned after the fall of Bukhara, receives dignitaries. MS. Suppl. Persan 1113, folio 90 recto. Courtesy Bibliothèque Nationale, Paris.

6 The inhabitants of Balkh leave the city after its surrender. MS. No. D 31 of Rashid-ad-Din, folio 85 recto. Courtesy Asiatic Society of Bengal, Calcutta and Warburg Institute, University of London.

7 Battle between armies of Chingis Khan and Jelal-ad-Din. MS. Suppl. Persan 1113, folio 72 recto. Courtesy Bibliothèque Nationale, Paris.

8   Chingis Khan's encampment or *ordu*. MS. Suppl. Persan 1113, folio 66 verso. Courtesy Bibliothèque Nationale, Paris.

9   The Mongols under command of Samukha Baghatur besiege Chung-tu. MS. Suppl. Persan 1113, folio 65 verso. Courtesy Bibliothèque Nationale, Paris.

10 The bier of Chingis Khan. MS. D 31, folio 90 verso. Courtesy Asiatic Society of Bengal and Warburg Institute.

11 Ögödei Khan seated with his two sons Güyük and Kadan. MS. Suppl. Persan 1113, folio 132 verso. Courtesy Bibliothèque Nationale, Paris.

12 The pavilion called Frashi at Karakorum. MS. No. D 31, folio 21 verso. Courtesy Asiatic Society of Bengal and Warburg Institute.

13 Portrait of Ögödei Khan in the Imperial Portrait Gallery, Peking. Courtesy Percival David Foundation, London: from original portrait shown in the International Exhibition of Chinese Art 1935-6.

14 Portrait of the ageing Kubilai Khan in the Imperial Portrait Gallery, Peking.

15 Kubilai Khan crossing a river on a bridge of boats during the conquest of southern China. MS. No. D 31, folio 105 recto. Courtesy Asiatic Society of Bengal and Warburg Institute.

16 Hülegü feasts before leaving Mongolia to invade Iran. MS. No. D 31, folio 120 recto. Courtesy Asiatic Society of Bengal and Warburg Institute.

17 Hülegü advances to attack the assassins. Note the *tuk*, the standard of nine yaks' tails. MS. No. D 31, folio 55 verso. Courtesy Asiatic Society of Bengal and Warburg Institute.

18 Hülegü besieges Baghdad. The final phase: surrender of the Caliph during the bombardment. MS. Suppl. Persan 1113, folios 180 verso—181 recto.

19 The Mongols besiege a city on a river, with a bridge on which their commander-in-chief stands. The city is probably Baghdad. From MS. of Rashid-ad-Din, MS. Diez A, folio 70, older than the Paris MS. in Tübingen. Courtesy Staatsbibliothek Preussischer Kulturbesitz. Depot Tübingen.

20 Stampede of horses rushing against riders coming the opposite way while Mongols shoot at them from walls. MS. Diez A, folio 70. Courtesy Staatsbibliothek Preussischer Kulturbesitz. Depot Tübingen.

21 Prisoners led off by Mongol cavalry. They are fastened to branches of a tree attached to the rider's saddle, and will have to keep pace in this position with the horse. MS. Diez A, folio 70. Courtesy Staatsbibliothek Preussischer Kulturbesitz. Depot Tübingen.

22 Scene from Mongol Invasion Scroll (*Moko Shurai Ekotoba*). Champions Takezaki and the three Ogano brothers attack Mongol warship. Courtesy National Museum, Tokyo, and permission Vice-Grand-Chamberlain to H.I.M. the Emperor of Japan.

23 Scene from Mongol Invasion Scroll. Mongol warship attacked by Japanese. Courtesy National Museum, Tokyo, and permission Vice-Grand-Chamberlain to H.I.M. the Emperor of Japan.

24 Scene from Mongol Invasion Scroll in the Tokyo National Museum. The Japanese champion Takezaki attacks Mongol archers. Courtesy Tokyo National Museum, and permission Vice-Grand-Chamberlain to H.I.M. the Emperor of Japan.

25 Cavalry pursuit. From MS. of Rashid-ad-Din, Hazine 1653 p. 165 B in the Topkapi Sarayi Museum, Istanbul.

26 Battle between Tartar cavalry and some oriental army. From illustrated MS. of Hayton, *Floire des Estoires*. Codex No. 2623, folio 22 B. Courtesy Österreichische Staatsbibliothek, Vienna.

27 Battle on a bridge over the Danube between Hungarians and Tartars. From MS. Codex No. 2623, folio 290. Courtesy Österreichische Staatsbibliothek.

28 Scene from the Mongol invasion of Hungary. Mongols, not fully armed, in pursuit of King Bela of Hungary. Illumination from MS. of *The Chronicle of Marcus Kalti*, S XIV.

29 Another scene from the same MS. shows Mongols in ordinary dress with captive women. One draws his bow against some enemy, while Hungarian soldiers on foot seem to be held back from further fighting by a woman. The Mongols are not wearing helmets or other armour in either of these pictures, perhaps because of victory.

30 The Ilkhan Abaka and his son Arghun. MS. Suppl. Persan 1113, folio 198 verso. Courtesy Bibliothèque Nationale, Paris.

31 Arghun, son of Abaka, with two wives, Ghazan and brothers. MS. Suppl. Persan 1113, folio 203 verso. Courtesy Bibliothèque Nationale, Paris.

32 Mongol princes and courtiers of Ghazan Khan. Ghazan Khan, enthroned, with his wife Bulughan Khatun beside him and four others seated on sandali chairs. MS. Suppl. Persan 1113, folio 227 verso. Courtesy Bibliothèque Nationale, Paris.

33 The Ilkhan Gaikhatu Khan, enthroned, prepares to judge the generals who revolted after the death of Arghun. MS. Suppl. Persan 1113, folio 208 recto. Courtesy Bibliothèque Nationale, Paris.

34 The coffin of Ghazan Khan. MS. Suppl. Persan 1113, folio 245 verso. Courtesy Bibliothèque Nationale, Paris.

35 Borak Khan recognized as ruler of the *ulus* of Jaghatai. MS. D 31, folio 56 verso. Courtesy Asiatic Society of Bengal and Warburg Institute.

36 Heading of inscription in old Chinese seal character set up by Kubilai Khan to a Buddhist priest near the summer Palace of Shang-tu. After Yule and Cordier, *The Book of Ser Marco Polo,* Vol. I, facing p. 305.

37 Portrait of Khaishan Khan of the Yüan Dynasty in the Imperial Portrait Gallery, Peking. Courtesy Percival David Foundation.

38 Coins of the thirteenth to eighteenth centuries AD. Approx. 5 : 4.
British Museum, photo Brompton Studio.

(a) Silver coin of Chingis Khan, struck in Afghanistan *c.* 1220 (*cf.*
Fig. 17, p. 68).

(b) Silver coin of the Great Khans, struck in north-west Persia *c.* 1240
(*cf.* Fig. 20, p. 78).

(c–e) Silver coins struck at Tiflis (Georgia): (c) 1244–5, during the
regency of Queen Töregene (*cf.* Fig. 21, p. 79); (d) 1247, in the names
of Güyük Khan and David Narin (*cf.* Fig. 22, p. 80); (e) 1252–61, in
the name of Möngke (*cf.* Fig. 23, p. 89).

(f) Bronze coin of Hülegü, struck at Irbil (Mesopotamia) 1262–3 (*cf.*
Fig. 31, p. 117).

(g) Gold coin of Ghazan Mahmud, struck at Shiraz 1300–1 (*cf.* Fig. 32,
p. 121).

(h, i) Bronze coins struck at Mosul: (h) Coin of Hülegü *c.* 1263–4.
Obv. Diademed head to left. *Rev.* 'Ka'an, the Supreme, Mungka
Khan—Hulagu Khan'. This wording shows Hülegü as subject to
Möngke. (i) Coin of Abaka 1274–5. *Obv.* Figure seated cross-legged,
holding a crescented moon in his uplifted hands. *Rev.* 'Ka'an, the
Supreme—Abagha, Ilkhan, the Great—may their might be increased'.
This form of words still shows Abaka as vassal of the Great Khan.

(j) Bronze coin of Öljeitü, struck at Baghdad 1312–3. *Obv.* Mint, date.
Around: 'There is no god but Allah, Muhammad is the Messenger of
Allah'. *Rev.* Lion passant, to left, beneath a sun. Around: 'The
Supreme Sultan Uljaitu Sultan, may God perpetuate his kingdom'.
No more mention of the Great Khan; this had been dropped by
Ghazan.

(k) Bronze coin of Abu Sa'id 1316–35, mint and date illegible. *Obv.*
'The Supreme Sultan Abu Sa'id, may God perpetuate his kingdom'.
Rev. Lion passant, to left, beneath a sun.

(l) Silver coin of Shahin Girai, Khan of the Crimea 1777–83, struck
at Baghche Sarai. *Obv.* Monogram of Khan. *Rev.* Tamgha of the
Krim Khans. Below, mint and accession date. One of the very latest
Mongol coins in existence.

39 Defeat of Tokhta by Nogai on the banks of the Don. MS. D 31, folio
44 recto. Courtesy Asiatic Society of Bengal and Warburg Institute.

Index

PERSONS AND PEOPLES

Abaka (Abagha, Abaqa), Ilkhan, 119–120, 122–130
Abd-ar-Rahman, minister, 79
Abu'l Faraj (Gregory Bar Hebraeus), historian, 17
Abu'l Ghazi Bahadur Khan, historian, 17
Abu Sa'id, Ilkhan, 122, 123–4
Abu 'Umar Menhaj-ad-Din al Juzjani (Juzjani), historian, 17
Adam of Salimbene, historian, 18
Ahmed (Tekuder), Ilkhan, 120
Ahmed, Khan of Kipchak, 135
Aibek, envoy, 83, 89
Ai-tsung, Chin emperor, 67, 70
Alans, 63
Alexander Nevsky, 129
Alexander of Lithuania, 130
Alfonso of Aragon, 130
Alghuy, Jaghatai khan, 125, 126
Aligirdas, Grand Duke of Lithuania, 131
Ali Sultan, Jaghatai khan, 126
Aljai Temür, 140
Al Malik al Nasir, Mameluk sultan, 120
Altaic peoples and languages, 21
Altan Khan, Mongol ruler, 141
Amasandji, Mongol khan, 141
Ambakhai, Mongol khan, 25
André de Longjumeau, friar, 83
Ao Tun-hiang, Chin general, 55

Arabshah, Kipchak pretender, 132
Arghun, Ilkhan, 120, 122
Arik Böge, Mongol prince, 86, 87, 88, 104, 125–6
Arpa, Ilkhan general, 131
Arslan, Khan of Karluks, 52
Ascelin (Ezzelino), friar, 83
Ashagambu, Tangut general, 52, 60, 65
Asikipa, Yüan emperor, 113
Assassins, Order of, 88
Atziz, Khwarazmshah, 58
Ayusidhara, Yüan prince, 114, 140

Baibars, Mameluk sultan, 115, 116, 119, 130
Baidu, Ilkhan, 122, 123
Baiju, Mongol general, 72, 80, 83, 90
Barak, Mongol chief, 134
Barchuk, Idikut of the Uighurs, 52
Batu Khan, 65, 69; invades Russia, 81; his *ulus*, 127–9
Bayan, general of Kubilai, 105; Mongol minister under Yüan, 113, 114
Bela, King of Hungary, 74
Benedict, friar, 18
Berdibeg, Khan of Kipchak, 124, 132
Berke, Khan of Kipchak, 115, 117, 126, 129
Böge, Ilkhan vizier, 122
Böge Temür, 90
Borak, Jaghatai khan, 119, 126
Borjigin, clan, 25
Börtei, wife of Chingis, 66

198

Boru, Mongol general, 67
Bridia, C. de, friar, 18
Bughra, Ibn Khafraj, envoy, 60
Bulgars, on the Kama, 65, 69, 72, 133; in the Balkans, 75, 130
Buriyat, Mongol tribe, 26, 51
Burundai, general under Berke, 129
Buyantu, Yüan emperor, 113
Buzar, King of Almalik, 52

Carpini, John de Plano, friar and historian, 18, 33, 80; his mission, 81–3
Casimir III of Poland, 131
Casimir IV of Poland, 135–6
Chahar, Mongol tribe, 141
Chang Chun, sage, 67
Chapar, son of Kaidu, 126
Charles of Anjou, 130
Ch'ien-lung Ch'ing emperor, 143
Chiluku, Gurkhan of Karakhitai, 57
Chin, Dynasty of China, 15, 23, 25; annals of, 25, 51; attacked by Chingis, 53; attacked by Ögödei, 70–1
Chinese, 22; their inventions in war, 60–1
Ch'ing Dynasty of China, 141
Chingis Khan (Jenghiz Khan), 14, 16, 25; proclamation of Temujin as, 39–40; organises state and army, 40–5; invades Tangut, 52; invades Chin Empire, 53–8 invades Khwarazmian Empire, 58–63; destroys Tangut, 65–6; dies, 66; historical importance, 67, 144
Choban, Ilkhan general, 120, 121, 124, 131
Chormagan, Mongol general, 71, 72, 90
Choros, division of Oïrat, 140, 142

Chu Yüan-chang (Hung Wu), founder of Ming Dynasty, 114
Cumans, 72, 75

Daniel of Galich, 129
David V of Georgia, 117
David VI of Georgia, 120
David, envoy, 84
Dayan, Mongol khan, 141
Devlet Berdi, Tartar chief, 134
Dewatdar, the Little, (Munjahid-ad-Din Aibek), Caliph's minister, 89, 90
Dimitri, Grand Duke, 132
Dokuz Khatun (Doquz), wife of Hülegü, 119
Dörböt, tribe of Oïrat, 140, 142

Edigü, Tartar chief, 132–4
Edward I of England, 112
Elbek, Mongol khan, 140
Eljigidei, Mongol commander, 83, 84
Esen Böge, Jaghatai khan, 126
Esen Taiji, Khan of Oïrat, 141

Fei Yang-ku, Ch'ing general, 142
Frederick II, emperor, 84

Gaikhatu, Ilkhan, 122, 123
Galden, Khan of Zungars, 142
George IV of Armenia, 63
Ghazan, Ilkhan, 17, 119, 120, 122, 123
Ghurs, 62, 65
Girai Khans, 137 ff.
Golden Horde, 127–38
Go ong, Mongol title (= Chinese Kuo Wang), 57
Grand Dukes, Russian, 128, 130, 132; Lithuanian, 129, 132

Great Horde, in Russia, 135–7
Gregory of Akner, historian, 17
Güchlük, Naiman, chief, 58
Guichard of Cremona, friar, 83
Gurkhan, 52
Güyük Khan (Kuyuk, Keuchan), 72, 79–85

Hajji Sarkis, Kipchak pretender, 132
Hajji Girai, Khan in Crimea, 135
Hakazaki, Japanese warrior, 106
Han Dynasty of China, 22
Hayton (Hethum) of Armenia, 17, 80, 120
Henry of Silesia, Archduke, 75
Hiung⁄Nu, 22–3
Hu Heng, Chinese official, 109
Huan⁄tsung, Chin emperor, 55, 56, 58
Hülegü Khan, 88 ff., 115 ff.

Ibn⁄al⁄Athir, historian, 16
Idikut, Uighur title, 52
Ilkhans, 115–24, 129
Inalchik, 60, 61
Indravarman, of Champa, 107
Innocent IV, Pope, 18, 81
Ivan Kalita, Grand Duke, 131
Ivan III of Moscow, 135
Ivan IV of Moscow, 137

Jacob of Sicily, 130
Jaghatai, son of Chingis, 54, 62, 69, 125; his *ulus*, 116, 125–36, 142
Jalairs, 124
Jamuka, 37
Janibeg, Khan of Kipchak, 124, 131
Japanese, 106–7

Javanese, 108–9
Jebe, 37, 54–5, 58, 63, 65
Jelal⁄ad⁄Din, 16, 62, 63, 71–2
Jelme, 37
Jenkshi, Jaghatai khan, 126
Jews, 33
Jöchi, 51, 54, 61, 62, 65; his *ulus*, 69, 116
John of Montecorvino, historian, 112
Juan⁄Juan, 23
Juchen (Jürchet, Nuchen), 23, 54, 56, 60
Juvaini ('Ala⁄ad⁄Din 'Ata Malik al Juvaini) historian, 16

Kadan, Mongol chief, 72
Kaikobad, Seljuk sultan, 71
Kalawun, Mameluk sultan, 120
Kalmuk, Mongol tribe, 142
Kam (Mongol for Shaman), 33
Kamala, son of Kubilai, 113
Kang Hi, Ch'ing emperor, 142
Kara Hülegü, Jaghatai khan, 125
Karakhanids, 59
Karluks, 52, 60
Kerait, Mongol tribe, 25, 26, 37, 38
Kepek, 134
Ke⁄shi⁄lie Chih⁄chung, Chin general, 54
Ketböge, Mongol general, 88, 90, 115–6
Khaishan, Yüan emperor, 113
Khalka, Mongol tribe, 141
Khasar, 38, 69
Khitan, 23, 52, 60
Khochot, Mongol tribe, 140
Khongirat, Mongol tribe, 26
Khurshah (Rokn⁄ad⁄Din Khurshah) Shaykh of the Assassins, 89
Kia Sse⁄tao, Sung minister, 104–5

Kilij Arslan, Seljuk sultan, 80
Kipchak, 63, 65, 115, 116
Kirghiz, 51
Kokchü, Shaman, 40
Köpek, Jaghatai khan, 121, 126
Kotyan, Khan of the Cumans, 74
Kubilai Khan, 19, 86, 106–113
Küchük Mahmed, Tartar chief, 134
Kushala, Yüan emperor, 113
Kutlugh Shah, Ilkhan general, 120
Kutula, Mongol khan, 25
Kutuz, Mameluk sultan, 115–6

Li An-chüan, King of Tangut, 52
Liao dynasty of China, 16, 23, 52
Ligdan, Mongol khan, 141
Lin-an (Hang-chou), Sung capital, 87, 104, 105
Lithuanians, 75, 130–1, 135
Li-tsung, Sung emperor, 71, 87
Liu Ping-chung, scholar, 109
Louis IX of France, 18, 84, 91, 130
Louis of Portugal, friar, 81

Magyars, 82
Mahamu, Khan of the Oïrat, 140
Mahmud Yalavach, minister of Great Khans, 78, 79, 125
Mahmudek of Kazan, 134
Majd-al-Mulk, Ilkham vizier, 122
Mamai, Tartar chief, 132
Mameluks, 84, 115–6, 120, 129
Manchus, 23
Mandughai Khatun, 141
Mangkhol (Mongols), 26
Mengli Girai, Crimean khan, 135–7
Manghut, Mongol tribe, 130

Manichees, 110
Manuel, Byzantine emperor, 117
Mar Yaballaha, Nestorian patriarch, 17
Markus, envoy, 84
Markus, Nestorian monk, 112
Masud Beg, son of Mahmud Yalavach, 125
Matthew Paris, historian, 18
Meng-ku, Meng-wu (Chinese name for Mongols), 24–5
Merkit, Mongol tribe, 26, 28, 58
Michael VIII, Byzantine emperor, 117
Michael of Tver, 135
Ming Dynasty of China, 16, 115, 139–141
Mirkhond (Muhammad ibn Hawand Shah), historian, 17
Möngke Khan (Mangu), 18, 72, 85–91
Möngke Temür, Khan of Kipchak, 130
Mongols, 13–4, 20–1; their institutions, 24–35; their later history, 139–144
Mostassem, Caliph of Baghdad, 88, 89, 90
Mstislav of Galich, 65
Mubarak Shah, Jaghatai khan, 126
Muhammad-al-Nasawi, historian, 16
Muhammad (Ala-ad-Din Muhammad), Khwarazmshah, 58, 59–62
Muhammad (Ala-ad-Din Muhammad), Shaykh of the Assassins, 88
Mukali, 37, 56, 57, 66–7
Murteza, Khan of Great Horde, 136
Muwied-ad-Din ben Akami, vizier of Baghdad, 89

Nachigai (also called Itügen and Etügen), Mongol goddess, 34

Naiman, Mongol tribe, 26, 38
Nan jen, class of Chinese, 109
Narasihapati of Mien, 108
Nasir, Caliph of Baghdad, 59, 71
Nauruz, Ilkhan minister, 123
Nayan, Mongol khan, 109
Nestorians, 17, 26, 81
Nikephoros Gregoras, historian, 17
Nogai, Mongol prince, 119, 129–30
Nurhachi, Manchu conqueror, 141

Odoric of Pordenone, historian, 19
Ögödei Khan, 54, 62, 66, 69–79
Ogul Gaimysh, Queen Regent, 84
Oïrat (Dorben Oïrat, four confeder-
ates), Mongol tribe, 26, 140
Okin Barkak, Mongol chief, 25
Öljeitü (Oljaitu), Ilkhan, 120–1, 123
Öngüt, Turco-Mongol tribe, 26, 54, 55
Orda, brother of Batu, 128
Ottoman Turks, 116, 125, 132, 136–7,
143
Özbeg, Khan of Kipchak, 121–2, 131

Phagspa, Tibetan Lama, 110; script
invented by him, 110
Philip the Fair, of France, 112, 120
Ping, Sung child emperor, 105
Polo, Marco, historian, 18, 33
Prester John, 81

Rabban Sauma, Nestorian monk, 112
Rabban Ata, Nestorian bishop, 83
Rashid-ad-Din Fadl' Allah, historian,
15, 16–7, 123
Rubruck, William of, historian, 18, 33,
91, 94
Rusudani, Queen of Georgia, 72

Sad-ad-Daula, Ilkhan vizier, 122
Sa'id Ahmed, son of Tokhtamysh, 134–5
Sargis, envoy, 83
Sartakh, Khan of Kipchak, 129
Seljuk Turks, of Iran, 58
Seljuk Turks, of Rum, 71, 88, 117, 118
Sempad, Armenian marshal, 17
Sengüm, son of Toghrul, 37, 38
Shadibeg, Mongol khan, 134
Shan tribes, 86, 87
Shaykh Ahmed, Khan of Great Horde,
136
Shi, Sung child emperor, 105
Shi-wei tribes, 24
Shiban, brother of Batu, 128
Shibanid Khans, 142
Shigi Kutuku, 15, 62
Shi Tien-tse, Chinese general of Kubilai,
104–5
Shiramun, 79
Sien Pi, 23
Sihasura of Mien, 108
Si Liao dynasty of Karakhitai, 52
Simeon, Grand Duke, 131
Singtaur, son of Kubilai, 108
Sin Sie-ji, Governor of Ta-li, 108
Su Ta, Ming general, 114
Sübüdei, 37, 63, 70, 72, 144
Sudhipala, Yüan emperor, 113
Sügetü, (So-ta), Mongol general, 107–8
Suleiman Shah, Caliph's general, 90
Sung Dynasty of China, 15, 67, 70–1,
86–8, 104–5
Surkukteni (Seroctan), wife of Tolui, 85

Taj-ad-Din Alishah, Ilkhan vizier, 123
Takash, Khwarazmshah, 58

T'ang Dynasty of China, 16, 24, 52
Tangut, 52, 60, 65–6
Tarmashirin, Jaghatai khan, 126
Tartars, name of Mongols in Russia, 128
Tatars (Chinese Ta-ta), Mongol tribe, 25
Teleböge, Khan of Kipchak, 130
Temüge, 54, 65, 69
Temujin (later Chingis Khan), 37–8
Temür, son of Kubilai, 113
Temür Kutlugh, 133
Tengri, Mongol god, 34
Thai tribes, 86–7
Tibetans, 52, 65
Timur (Tamerlane), 13, 132, 139
Timur Khan, Kipchak pretender, 134
Timur Kutlugh, Kipchak pretender, 134
Toba, 23
Togan, son of Kubilai, 108
Togha Temür, brother of Batu, 128
Toghan Temür (Shun-Ti), 113, 114
Toghon, son of Mahamu, 140
Toghrul Khan (Wang Khan) of the Kerait, 37–8
Togh Temür, Yüan emperor, 113, 114
Tokhta, Yüan minister, 114
Tokhta, Khan of Kipchak, 120, 130, 132–3
Tokhtamysh, Khan of Kipchak, 132–3
Tokur Temür, Mongol khan, 140
Tolui, youngest son of Chingis, 66, 69, 70
Töregene (Turakina), Queen Regent, 79
Törghüt, tribe of Oïrat, 140, 142
Tran Dynasty of Annam, 75, 87
Tran Thai-tong, king, 107

Tran Thanh-tong, king, 107
Tuan Vijaya, Javan king, 108
Tuda Möngke, Khan of Kipchak, 130
Tumet, Mongol tribe, 26, 51
Tung Ta-tsuan, Sung minister, 87
Tungus peoples, 23, 24
Turkish peoples, Turks (see also Otto-man and Seljuk), 21, 24
Turkhan Khatun, Queen, 59
Tuva, Jaghatai khan, 126

Ugetchi, Mongol khan, 140
Uighurs, 28, 53, 60
Ulugh Mahmed, son of Tokhtamysh, 134
Uriangkadai, son of Sübüdei, Mongol general, 86, 87
Urus Khan, 132

Vais, Jaghatai khan, 140
Vassili, Grand Duke, 133
Vincent of Beauvais, historian, 18
Vytautas (Vitovt, Witold), Grand Duke of Lithuania, 133, 134

Wan-yen Hu-sha, Chin general, 54
Wassaf (Ibn Fadl' Allah), historian, 17
Wei Shao Wang, Chin emperor, 54, 55
Wenceslas of Bohemia, 75

Yagailo (Jagellon) of Poland, 133
Yao Chi, scholar, 86
Yao Shu, scholar, 109
Yang Lo, Ming emperor, 140
Yasavur, Jaghatai khan, 121, 126
Ye-liu Chu-tsai, Khitan, statesman and minister of Chingis, 57, 58–9, 67, 70

Ye-liu Tai-shi, Khitan, founder of Si-
Liao Dynasty, 52, 68
Ye-liu Tukha, Khitan general, 54
Yesügei, father of Chingis, 25
Yesu Möngke, Jaghatai khan, 125
Yesun Temür, Yüan emperor, 113
Yesun Timur, Jaghatai khan, 126
Yuri, Grand Duke, 72
Yüan dynasty of China, 15, 104–15

PLACES, COUNTRIES AND
GEOGRAPHICAL FEATURES

Afghanistan, 61, 62, 65
'Ain Jalut, Battle of, 115
Alamut, fortress, 88
Ala Shan Mts, 52, 65
Alatagh Mt, 118
Albania, Balkan, 75
Albania, Transcaucasian, 72
Aleppo, 91
Almalik, 52, 126
Altai Mts, 20, 61
Amu Darya, R., 62, 67
Amur, R., 20, 143
Ani, 72
An-hui, 104
Annam, 87, 107, 108, 113
Armenia, Greater, 63, 71–2, 118
Armenia, Lesser, 118, 119
Arran, 88
Astrakhan, 132, 133
Azerbaijan, 63, 71, 88, 90, 117

Baalbek, 83
Baghdad, 63, 89, 90
Baikal, L., 20, 26, 141

Balasaghun, 52
Baljuna, L., 38
Balkash, L., 61, 141
Balkh, 61, 63
Bamiyan, 62
Bishbalik, 52
Breslau, 75
Bukhara, 61, 119, 125
Burkhan Kaldun Mt, 33
Buyur Nor, L., 25, 26, 140

Carpathian Mts., 74
Caucasia, Caucasus, 127, 131, 132, 133
Ceylon, 109
Champa, 107, 113
Cheng-tu, 88
Chernigov, 128
China, 20, 25, 53–8, 66–8, 70–1, 85–8,
104–15
Ching Chou, 54
Chmielnik, 74
Chü Yung Kuan, fortress, 55
Chung Kuo (Middle Kingdom, China),
166
Chung-tu, 54–6, 104
Crimea, 19, 63, 130–1, 135
Croatia, 75

Dalmatia, 75
Damascus, 91
Damghan, 71
Derbend, 63, 117
Dniepr, R., 65
Dolon Nur, L., 87
Don, R., 72

Emba, R., 142
Erdeni Tzu, 143

Erijayu, 65
Erikaya (Chung Sing), 52, 66

Fan-cheng, fortress, 104
Fars, 88, 118
Fu-kien, 105

Galicia (Galich), 128
Georgia, 63, 72, 88, 118
Ghaznah, 62
Gilan, 118
Gobi Desert, 20, 22, 54
Gran, 74
Grand Canal, 112
Great Wall, 54
Gurganj, 62

Hamadan, 63
Han, R., 104
Hanoi, 108
Herat, 63, 88, 118
Hi-ching, 55
Ho-lin (Karakorum), 96
Homs, 120
Honan, 66, 86
Hopei, 56, 66, 86
Hormuz, 118
Ho-chou, 88
Huai, R., 104
Huan chou, 54
Huan-er-tsi, 54, 55
Huang Ho, 20, 52, 55, 57, 58, 65–6, 70
Hungary, 20, 74

Iki, 106
Ili, R., 52, 125, 140, 142
Imeretia, 72
Imil (Omyl), 84, 142
India, 109

Iran, 63, 69, 71–2, 88
Iraq, 71–2
Iraq el Adjem, 88
Irawaddy, R., 108
Irtysh, R., 60
Ispahan, 71

Japan, 106–7
Java, 108–9
Jejer-ündür, Battle of, 38

Kaffa, 128, 132
Kalakaljit-elet, Battle of, 38
Kalka, R., 65, 132
Kama, R., 74
Kamakura, 106
Kansu, 51
Karakhitai, 52, 58
Karakorum, 19, 24, 85, 86, 87, 91,
    94–103, 125
Kars, 72
Kashgaria, 142, 143
Kasvin, 63
Kaung-sin, 108
Kerman, 71, 118
Kertch, 128
Kerulen, R., 20, 25, 38, 142
Khingan Mts, 20, 26, 38, 54
Khurasan, 58, 71, 88, 118–31
Khwarazm, 57, 127, 131
Kiang-chou, 106
Kiang-si, 105
Kiao-chi, 87
Kien-kang, 105
Kiev, 74, 128
King-shan Mts, 87
Kizil Kum Desert, 61

Kolomna, 72
Kopistryn, Battle of, 136
Korea, 57, 71, 106, 107
Köse Dagh, Battle of, 80
Kuangsi, 87, 105
Kuang-tung, 105
Kuei-te, 70
Kulikovo, Battle of, 132
Kun-chou, 70
Kura, R., 63, 117, 129
Kyushu, 106

Lin-an (Hang-chou), 87, 104, 105
Lithuania, 75, 130–1, 135
Lo-yang, 70
Lung-kang, 87, 88
Lung-kiang, 87
Luristan, 118
Lyons, 81

Maimundiz, fortress, 89
Malabar, 107
Manchuria, 20, 25, 57, 69
Maragha, 124
Mazenderan, 71
Merv, 63
Mien, 108, 113
Mohi, 75
Mongolia, 13, 20
Moscow, 72, 132, 133
Mosul, 83, 117
Mu Cheng, fortress, 108
Mughan Steppe, 63, 118
Murom, 128

Nerchinsk, Treaty of, 143
Nizhny Novgorod, 133
Novgorod, 74, 128

Oka, R., 74
Onon, R., 26
Ordos Desert, 20, 51, 67
Orkhon, R., 24, 26, 80, 142

Palaces, at Karakorum, 94, 100–3; at
   Ta-tu, 112; at Shang-tu, 113
Parwan, Battle of, 62
Pei-chou, 70
Pereyaslavl, 128
Pereyaslavl Zalessky, 72
Pesth, 74
Pinsk, 128
Podolia, 74
Poland, 74, 130
Polotsk, 128
Prussia, 75

Qais, 118

Rostov, 72, 128
Russia, 72–4
Ryazan, 72, 128, 133

Samarkand, 61–2, 125, 132, 139
Sarai, Old, 19, 128; New, 19, 128,
   132–3, 137–8
Sayo, R., 75
Selenga, R., 20, 24, 26
Semirechye, 125
Serbia, 75–6
Seversk, 128
Shabankara, 118
Shakkab, Battle of, 120
Shang-tu (Xanadu), 87, 113
Shansi, 66, 67
Shantung, 56
Shensi, 67

Shiraz, 71
Shirvan, 63
Siang-yang, fortress, 104–5
Sien, 107
Si-Hia, 51
Sit, R., 72
Smolensk, 128
Ssechuan, 86–7
Sudak, 128
Sultaniye, 123
Suzdal, 72, 128
Syr Darya, R., 58, 61

Tabriz, 83, 117, 131
Tagaung, 108
Ta-li, 86
Ta-liang (Kai-feng), 56, 57, 70
Tarim, R., 52, 125, 141
Ta-tu (Chung-tu renamed), 104, 112
Te-hing-chou, 55
Terek, R., 133
Theiss, R., 75
Tibet, 62, 65
Tiflis, 63, 71, 72
T'ien Shan Mts., 20
Transoxiana, 17, 52, 58, 120–1, 127, 132, 133, 139
Tsushima, 106
Tu Sung Kuan, fortress, 105
Tung-ching, 55
Tung Kuan, fortress, 57
Tver, 72
Tzu Ching Kuan, fortress, 55

Ukraine, 63, 74
Urahai, 52
Urga (Ulan-bator), 142–3

Urungu, R., 142
Utrar, 60, 61

Venice, 128, 130
Vladimir, 72
Volga, 19, 63
Volhynia, 74, 128

Wahlstatt, Battle of, 75
Wei, R., 70

Yang-chou, 104
Yangtse, R., 86–7
Yaroslavl, 72
Ye-hu-ling Mts., 54
Ying-tien Mts., 114
Yunnan, 86–7

Zarafshan, R., 61
Zungaria, 22, 52, 88, 142

SUBJECTS AND TERMS

administration, Mongol, 76
Altan Debter, 15
Altan Tobchi, 15
altan uruk, 40
anda, 27
arban, 40, 44
armour, 45–6
army, 42–5, 49–50
ayil, 30

baghatur, 26
bakufu, 106
baskaks, 78, 119, 128
boyars, 128
burial, 33

camels, 28
chen-shu, 110

darkhan (pl. darkhat), 24, 27
darughachis, 78, 128
dinar, 118
dirham, 118
dress, Mongol, 31–2

equipment, military, 47–8

fedayin, 88
food, Mongol, 28

ger, 30

han-jen, 109
hunting, Mongol, 42

idols, Mongol, 30–1
idzhi, 99
inju (pl. inje), 76
irgen, 26

jalaghu, 26
jegun, 40

kalan, 78
kara'ul, 50
kebte'ut, 42
keshik, 42, 44
khan, 24
khatun, 24
kopchur, 78
korchi, 42
kubi, 76
kumiss, 28
kuriltai, 38, 66, 69, 71, 80, 85, 88

maikhan, 30
mingan, 40

nan-jen, 109
nökür (pl. nököt), 27, 34
nomads, nomadism, 21–4
noyan (pl. noyat), 27, 40, 76, 78

obok, 26
ongon (pl. ongot), 34
ordu, 24
otole bogol, 26

paitza (pl. paitze), 78
paper money, 112, 123

religion, Mongol, 33–5

se-mu-jen, 109
shogun, 106
sulde, 40

ta meng-ku kuo, 25
tamga, 78
tents, Mongol, 28–31
tuk, 40
tümen, 25, 40
turga'ut, 42

ulus, 24, 26, 69
unagan bogol, 27
uruk, 26

weapons, Mongol, 45

yam, 78, 112
yarlyk, 15
yasa, 15, 40–2
yasun, 26
yurt, 30

44143